Faszination Steinhuder Meer

Für meine Tochter Henrike
To my daughter Henrike

*Hauke Jagau
President of the
Hannover Region.*

*Dear Reader,
A visit to Lake Steinhude, no matter how short, will always create a feeling of vacation. And while the German name "Steinhuder Meer" literally translates as "Sea Steinhude", it is, of course, not a sea, but rather the largest inland lake in North-West Germany with an average water depth of 1.35 metres. But those who have been to Lake Steinhude know: With these waters, we have a true natural paradise and an El Dorado for water sports in the Hannover Region. It is not without reason that the lake has one of the longest traditions as a sailing area in Germany. At the same time, it is the heart of the Lake Steinhude Nature Reserve and thus a resting and breeding ground for thousands and thousands of birds.
This illustrated book that includes photographs taken by Heinrich K.-M. Hecht shows the diversity and the special beauty of this area of unspoiled nature. It shows us magnificent pictures that illustrate the treasure Lake Steinhude is holding for us. And it leaves you with the wish to take a little break and visit this landscape situated in the north-west of the Hannover Region.*

I hope you enjoy reading and paging through the book, and let yourself be inspired by the "feeling of the sea".

Hauke Jagau
Präsident der Region Hannover.

Liebe Leserinnen und Leser,
ein Besuch am Steinhuder Meer, und sei er auch noch so kurz, gibt einem immer ein Gefühl von Urlaub. Und das, obwohl es sich genau genommen nicht um ein Meer, sondern um Nordwestdeutschlands größten Binnensee mit einer durchschnittlichen Wassertiefe von 1,35 Metern handelt. Aber wer das Steinhuder Meer kennt, weiß: Wir haben mit diesem Gewässer im Westen der Region Hannover ein wahres Naturparadies und ein Dorado für den Wassersport. Nicht umsonst gehört der See zu den traditionsreichsten Segelrevieren in Deutschland. Zugleich ist es als Herzstück des Naturparks Steinhuder Meer Rast- und Brutgebiet für Abertausende von Vögeln.
Der vorliegende Bildband mit Fotos von Heinrich K.-M. Hecht zeigt die Vielfalt und die besondere Schönheit dieses Naturraums. Er führt uns in großartigen Aufnahmen vor Augen, welchen Schatz wir mit dem Steinhuder Meer haben. Und er macht Lust auf den nächsten Besuch, eine kleine Auszeit im Nordwesten der Region Hannover.

Ich wünsche Ihnen viel Spaß und „Meergefühl" beim Lesen und Blättern!

Why do we love Lake Steinhude?

Sitting at the lake with our parents in the evening and enjoying the sunset is simply great. In front of the Großenheidorn Sailors' Club we can even eat our Chicken Nuggets while looking at the sparkling water.

In summer, one can glide over the water on a sailing boat while admiring the animals and the landscape. It is simply wonderful when we go swimming off the landing stage with many friends, jump in, splashing all around, and swim a bit on the wide lake. Or splashing our parents, that's also a lot of fun ... We enjoy being in the company of friends and family.

Sometimes, with our surfboards, we just hold on to an electric boat and let it pull us – that's great and you don't have to do anything. Climbing on the trees on the property of the Lake Steinhude Yacht Club is also real fun. But we are careful and watch our steps as we don't want to hurt the trees. We enjoy the flowers that are already blooming beautifully in spring.

Dear adults, please join in and help to make sure that Lake Steinhude and its surroundings stay as beautiful as they are now.
Yours,
Mimi, Henriette & Henrike

Warum lieben wir das Steinhuder Meer?

Wenn wir abends mit unseren Eltern am Meer sitzen und den Sonnenuntergang genießen, dann ist das einfach nur toll. Vor dem Segler-Verein Großenheidorn können wir dabei sogar unsere Chicken Nuggets essen und auf das glitzernde Wasser schauen.

Im Sommer kann man mit Segelbooten über das Wasser rauschen und dabei noch die Tiere und Natur beobachten. Richtig schön ist es, wenn wir mit vielen Freunden vom Steg aus Baden gehen, rein springen, dass es nur so spritzt und ein wenig raus schwimmen. Die Eltern nass spritzen macht auch viel Spaß ... Es ist schön, wenn die Freunde und Familie zusammen sind.

Manchmal hängen wir uns auch mit einem Surfbrett hinter ein Elektroboot und lassen uns einfach nur ziehen – das ist super und man muss nichts tun. Aber klettern in den Bäumen auf dem Grundstück vom Yachtclub Steinhuder Meer ist auch gut. Wir passen aber auch auf und sind ganz vorsichtig, dass wir den Bäumen nicht wehtun. Wir erfreuen uns auch an den Blumen die im Frühling so schön blühen. Liebe Erwachsene, helft bitte alle mit, dass es am Steinhuder Meer so schön bleibt wie es ist.

Eure
Mimi, Henriette & Henrike

Faszination

Steinhuder Meer

Fascination Lake Steinhude

Von Heinrich K.-M. Hecht
By Heinrich K.-M. Hecht

www.HeinrichHecht.de

Inhalt
Contents

Geschichte
History

13

FASZINATION STEINHUDER MEER
FASCINATION LAKE STEINHUDE

Wilhelmstein	**Meer Handwerk**	**Naturpark & Moor**	**Meer Sport**	**Orte am Meer**
Wilhelmstein	Crafts at the lake	Nature Reserve & Moor	Sports by the lake	Towns & Villages by the lake

33   **49**   **69**   **111**   **147**

Danksagung	Über die Autoren	Partner und Sponsoren	Bildhinweise	Impressum
Thanks	About the authors	Partners and sponsors	Photo credits	Legal information

198   200   204   208   209

Geschichte

Text: Klaus Fesche

History

Der Sage nach entstand das Steinhuder Meer aus dem Fußabdruck von Riesen, die sich stritten und dabei Zwerge platt traten. Der endlose Tränenfluss der hinterbliebenen Zwerge füllten den großen Fussabdruck. Die Naturwissenschaft hingegen erklärt die Entstehung des größten niedersächsischen Sees als Folge der letzten Eiszeit – ausführlicher nachzulesen im Kapitel „Naturpark".
Wohl schon vor Ende der Eiszeit siedelten sich Menschen rund ums Steinhuder Meer an, wie viele Bodenfunde – Gräber, Keramiken, Werkzeuge und Waffen – belegen. Auch mehrere Einbäume wurden gefunden; zwei von ihnen sind im Turm der Festung Wilhelmstein ausgestellt. Sie zeigen, dass die Seeansiedler schon vor Tausenden von Jahren das Meer befuhren – sein Fischreichtum bot eine wertvolle Nahrungsgrundlage. Auch Enten und andere Wasservögel dürften den Speiseplan der Uferbewohner bereichert haben. Für das Tote Moor ist eine Nutzung erst seit dem 17. Jahrhundert belegt; eine Karte des schaumburg-lippischen Offiziers Praetorius von 1770 bezeichnet es als eine „morastige Wüste". Lediglich an seinem Südrand hatten die Einwohner verschiedener Dörfer und der Städte Neustadt und Wunstorf Handtorfstiche.
Mitte des 18. Jahrhunderts wurde ein Torfkanal zur Leine gegraben, um über diesen Weg Hannover mit Brenntorf zu versorgen.

Legend has it that Lake Steinhude was created from the footprint of giants who had an argument, stamping some dwarves down. The large footprint was then filled by the endless stream of tears of the dwarves left behind. Natural scientists, however, explain that the largest lake in Lower Saxony was created as a result of the last Ice Age – read more about this in the Chapter "Nature Reserve".
Probably already before the end of the Ice Age, people settled around Lake Steinhude, as can be proven by many archaeological finds – graves, ceramics, tools and weapons. Several dugout canoes were also found; two of these are exhibited in the tower of Wilhelmstein fortress. From these we know that people living in the shore regions already travelled on the lake thousands of years ago – the abundant fish was an important staple food. Ducks and other water birds are also likely to have added variety to the diet of the people living along the shore. The first proofs of exploitation of the Dead Moor date back to the 17th century. On a map drawn by Officer Praetorius of Schaumburg-Lippe around 1770, it is described as a "swampy desert". The inhabitants of various villages and of the towns Neustadt and Wunstorf dug for peat only at its southern border.
In the mid-18th century, a peat canal was dug to the Leine River as a supply route for transporting fuel peat to Hannover.

Improvisation ist alles: Bevor die „Auswanderer" die „Fremden" übers Meer beförderten, stellte man einfach Stühle in die Torfkähne
Improvisation is everything: Before the "Auswanderer" boats (see page 166) transported the "strangers" over the Lake, people simply put chairs in the peat barges

Während des Mittelalters bildeten sich allmählich die Herrschaftsräume aus, an deren Säumen das Steinhuder Meer gelegen war. Zunächst erwarben die Mindener Bischöfe und das Kloster Loccum Rechte bzw. Ländereien im Bereich des Sees, bevor weltliche Herren wie die Grafen von Roden, die Herzöge von Braunschweig-Lüneburg und die Grafen von Schaumburg zu ihnen und miteinander in Konkurrenz traten.

Bereits 798 war das Bistum Minden durch Karl den Großen gegründet worden, das seine Missionsarbeit auf das Gebiet ums Steinhuder Meer erstreckte und zu dem auch das 871 erstmals erwähnte Stift Wunstorf gehörte. Diesem standen laut einer Urkunde aus dem Jahre 1228 die Rechte am Fisch- und Vogelfang am und im Steinhuder Meer zu. Aus weiteren Urkunden der Folgezeit ist auch der erste uns bekannte Name des Gewässers überliefert: „Meer bei Wunstorf". Schon lange vor Steinhude wird Mardorf (=Meerdorf) 1173 erstmals urkundlich erwähnt. Steinhude taucht erst in einer 1290-1300 zu datierenden Urkunde auf.

Rund 200 Meter westlich vom heutigen Steinhuder Ufer wurden Reste einer Burgstelle gefunden, die lange Zeit mit der „Kranenburg" identifiziert wurde. Diese wird in einem Vertrag aus dem Jahre 1320 zwischen Herzog Otto von Braunschweig-Lüneburg und Graf Adolf VIII. von Schaumburg genannt. Neuesten Erkenntnissen von Burgenforschern und Archäologen zufolge ist diese Gleichsetzung jedoch nicht haltbar.

During the Middle Ages, realms bordering on Lake Steinhude developed. Initially, the bishops of Minden and the monastery of Loccum purchased ownership rights and estate in the area of the lake; later, secular sovereigns, such as the Counts of Roden, the Dukes of Braunschweig-Lüneburg and the Counts of Schaumburg competed with these and with each other over the land.

As early as 798, Charles the Great founded the Bishopric of Minden, which extended its missionary work to the area surrounding Lake Steinhude and which also included the Wunstorf monastery, first mentioned in 871. According to an official document from the year 1228, the latter held the fishery and bird hunting rights at and in Lake Steinhude. Other records from the time after that also included the initial name of the waters known to us: "Meer bei Wunstorf", meaning the "Sea near Wunstorf". Long before Steinhude, in 1173, Mardorf (=Meerdorf, meaning "village by the sea") was first mentioned in official documents.

Steinhude is first mentioned in a document dated around 1290-1300. Approximately 200 metres to the west of what is Lake Steinhude's shore today, remnants of a castle were discovered that, for a long time, were believed to stem from the "Kranenburg". The latter is mentioned in a contract concluded between Duke Otto von Braunschweig-Lüneburg and Count Adolf VIII in 1320.

Recent findings by castle researchers and archaeologists, however, disagree with this.

Die ersten genauen Landkarten des Steinhuder Meeres und seiner Umgebung schuf der bei Graf Wilhelm in Diensten stehende Offizier und Ingenieur Jakob Chrysostomus Praetorius; diese hier stammt aus dem Jahr 1770
Jakob Chrysostomus Praetorius, officer and engineer in the services of Count Wilhelm, drew the first accurate maps of Lake Steinhude and its surroundings; this one dates back to 1770

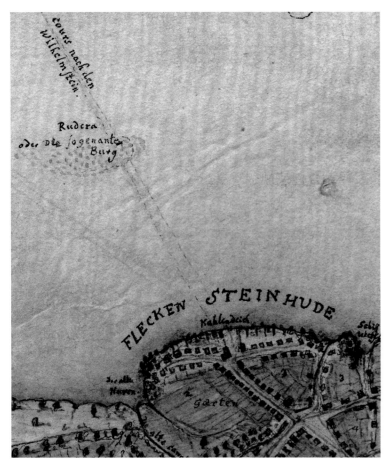

Auch die Karte von 1768, aus der dieser Steinhude zeigende Ausschnitt stammt, wurde von Praetorius angefertigt
This map from 1768, which is showing excerpt of Steinhude, was also drawn by Praetorius

Noch im 20. Jahrhundert stießen Steinhuder Schiffer wiederholt auf Burgreste, und die entsprechende Stelle im Meer wird schlicht „Burg" genannt. Im 14. und 15. Jahrhundert gelang es den Grafen von Schaumburg, ihre Herrschaft auf das Gebiet des Steinhuder Meeres auszudehnen und zu befestigen. Graf Erich verlieh den Steinhudern 1477 das Recht auf einen (abgabe-)freien Ratskeller, womit gleichzeitig die rund 500 Jahre währende kommunale Sonderstellung Steinhudes begründet wird: Der Ort war kein Bauerndorf, sondern ein sogenannter Flecken – ein Ort mit einer Zwischenstellung zwischen Dorf und Stadt, von einem Rat mit einem Bürgermeister an der Spitze in gewissen Grenzen selbst verwaltet und mit Marktrecht ausgestattet. Diese hervorgehobene Position und die Lage direkt am Ufer des Sees, den nur die Steinhuder Fischer befahren durften, dürfte den heutigen Namen „Steinhuder Meer" hervorgebracht haben.

Well into the 20th century, mariners from Steinhude repeatedly found remnants of a castle, and the corresponding spot in the lake is simply referred to as "castle". In the 14th and 15th century, the Counts of Schaumburg successfully extended and strengthened their realm to the Lake Steinhude region. In 1477, Count Erich granted the citizens of Steinhude the right to operate a (duty) free town hall cellar, thus creating the foundation for the special municipal position of Steinhude, which was to last for about 500 years: The town was not a farmers' village, but rather a so-called "Flecken", which is similar to a market town and refers to a place that has a status between a village and a town, that is autonomously administered – within certain limits – by a council headed by a mayor holding market rights. This distinguished position together with the location directly on the shores of the lake that only fishermen from Steinhude were allowed to exploit, is most likely the origin of today's name "Lake Steinhude".

Blick in die Graf-Wilhelm-Straße mit Schweers-Harms Fischerhus in den 30er Jahren
View of Graf-Wilhelm-Straße, where the Schweers-Harms Fischerhus is located, in the 1930s

Die Grafen von Schaumburg, später die Fürsten von Schaumburg-Lippe, konnten in Grenzkonflikten und -verträgen jahrhundertelang ihre Hoheit über das Steinhuder Meer bewahren. Noch heute bezeugen Straßen- und Schulnamen oder der Wilhelmstein, dass Graf Wilhelm von Schaumburg-Lippe wie kein Zweiter vor oder nach ihm das Steinhuder Meer prägte. Der von ihm erbaute Wilhelmstein galt seit 1787 als „unüberwindliche Festung" und zog von Jahr zu Jahr größere Scharen von Besuchern an. Um 1800 waren es einige Hundert Besucher im Jahr, die ihre Neugier zur Insel brachte, darunter illustre Persönlichkeiten wie Napoleons Bruder Jérôme Bonaparte, Monarch des Königreichs Westphalen. Die Befreiungskriege gegen Napoleon ließen auch den Stern des preußischen Generals Gerhard von Scharnhorst erstrahlen, der das preußische Heer reorganisierte. Scharnhorst war im nahen Bordenau geboren und hatte seine militärische Ausbildung auf dem Wilhelmstein erlangt – ein weiterer Grund für den Mythos und die Anziehungskraft der Insel.

The Counts of Schaumburg, later the Dukes of Schaumburg-Lippe, could successfully maintain their sovereignty over Lake Steinhude through border conflicts and border contracts. To this day, names of streets and schools or Wilhemstein fortress are proof that Count Wilhelm von Schaumburg-Lippe shaped Lake Steinhude like no one else before or after him. Since 1787, Wilhelmstein fortress built by him had been considered an "impregnable fortress", attracting an increasing number of visitors year after year. Around 1800, a few hundred visitors went to the island out of curiosity, among them famous people, such as Napoleon's brother Jérôme Bonaparte, Monarch of the Kingdom of Westphalia. The liberation wars against Napoleon also made the star of Prussian general Gerhard von Scharnhorst rise; he became known as the re-organizer of the Prussian army. Scharnhorst was born in nearby Bordenau, completing his military training on Wilhelmstein fortress – another reason that added to the myth and attraction of the island.

Rechts: Graf Wilhelm in der Uniform eines britischen Feldmarschalls. Er wurde von der englischen Krone nach dem Sieg über Frankreich/Spanien und der Rettung Portugals 1762 wegen hervorragender militärischer Leistungen zum Feldmarschall ernannt. Das Bild stammt von Johann Georg Ziesenis um 1770
Right: Count Wilhelm in the uniform of a British Field Marshal. After the victory over France/Spain and the saving of Portugal in 1762, the British Crown promoted him to Field Marshal in recognition of his outstanding military achievements. This picture was painted by Johann Georg Ziesenis around 1770

Begünstigt durch die Eisenbahn, die ab 1847 Reisende in die nahen Bahnhofsstädte, vor allem Wunstorf, beförderte, kamen um die Mitte des 19. Jahrhunderts schon Tausende „Fremde" auf die Insel. Als dann 1898 auch noch die Steinhuder Meer-Bahn (StMB) Steinhude und Hagenburg anfuhr, konnten bald fünfstellige Besucherzahlen auf dem Wilhelmstein registriert werden.

Benefited by the railway that transported travellers to the nearby railway station towns, first and foremost Wunstorf from 1847 on, thousands of "strangers" came to the island already in the mid-19th century. When in 1898 the Steinhuder Meer-Bahn (Lake Steinhude Railway, StMB) included Steinhude and Hagenburg on its route, the number of visitors to Wilhelmstein fortress soon reached five digit numbers.

Rechts: Eine unerschöpfliche Fundgrube stellen die Fremdenbücher des Wilhelmsteins dar. Sie wandelten sich von anfänglichen Besucherverzeichnissen zu Poesiealben, in die oft humorige Gedichte geschrieben und Bilder gezeichnet wurden. Eine besonders schöne Zeichnung stammt von August Meyer, mit der 1889 ein neues Fremdenbuch eingeleitet wurde
Right: The visitor books of Wilhelmstein fortress are an inexhaustible source of information. Initially nothing more than visitor registers, they later became true poetry books in which people wrote humorous poems and drawings. A particularly beautiful drawing by August Meyer was later used as introduction to a new visitors' book in 1889

Eine wichtige Rolle bei der Erschließung des Steinhuder Meeres für den Fremdenverkehr spielte die Steinhuder Meer-Bahn. Hier wird 1948 ihr 50-jähriges Jubiläum gefeiert
The Lake Steinhude Railway played an important role in the exploitation of Lake Steinhude as a tourist destination. This photograph shows its 50-year anniversary celebrated in 1948

Mit der StMB wurde das Steinhuder Meer endgültig zum Ziel des Fremdenverkehrs, der immer mehr Menschen ernährte. Waren es anfangs die „Fürstlichen Matrosen", die ihren Lebensunterhalt mit der Beförderung der Fremden zum Wilhelmstein verdienten, so gesellten sich nun auch zahlreiche Steinhuder Schiffer zu ihnen sowie mehr und mehr Gastronomen und die von ihnen Beschäftigten. Schon 1899 wurde das Strandhotel errichtet, von einer „Steinhuder-Meer-Gesellschaft", die den weiteren Ausbau des Fremdenverkehrs am Meer anstrebte und die bald auch ein erstes Motorschiff betrieb. Auch ein „Luft-, Licht- und Seebad" nach dem Muster der sonst eher in Großstädten gegründeten und den Zielen der Reformbewegung verpflichteten Einrichtungen wurde errichtet.

With the StMB, Lake Steinhude finally became a tourist destination, providing a source of income for more and more people. Initially, only the "Princely Sailors" earned their living by transporting tourists to Wilhelmstein. But soon, numerous mariners from Steinhude and also restaurant owners and their employees discovered the great potential. As early as 1899, the beach hotel was built by a certain "Lake Steinhude Society", which aimed to extend tourism at the Lake and soon started operating the first motor boat. An "Air, Light and Lakeside Resort", modelled after the facilities normally found only in large towns and designed according to the goals of the reformation movement, was also created.

In den ersten Jahrzehnten waren nur die Fürstlichen Matrosen befugt, Touristen zum Wilhelmstein zu bringen. Dieses Foto dürfte kurz vor dem Ersten Weltkrieg entstanden sein
In the first few decades, only the Princely Sailors had the right to transport tourists to Wilhelmstein. This photograph was probably taken shortly before the First World War

Schon vor der Wende zum 20. Jahrhundert setzten vereinzelt erste private Segelboote weiße Tupfer auf die Wasserfläche, denen nach einigen Jahren frühe Segelvereinsgründungen folgten: 1906 der Hagenburger (ab 1933 Hannoversche) Yachtclub (HYC), 1908 der Fürstlich Schaumburg-Lippische Seglerverein (ab 1937 Schaumburg-Lippischer Seglerverein, SLSV). Sie waren Vorboten zahlreicher Segelclubs in den nachfolgenden Jahrzehnten. Bald wurden national und international bedeutsame Regatten auf dem Meer gefahren.

Auch die touristische Eroberung des Nordufers begann in diesen Jahren. Wandervögel und andere Pioniere auf der Suche nach der „unberührten Natur" landeten am Weißen Berg und zogen bald weitere Besucher nach sich. Mit Ausbruch des Ersten Weltkriegs gingen die Besucherzahlen stark zurück, manche Betriebe überlebten den Krieg nicht.

Already before the turn to the 20th century, the first few private sailing boats painted white dots on the water surface, which was followed by the foundation of the first sailing clubs a few years later: The Hagenburg (from 1933 on, Hannover) Yacht Club (HYC) was established in 1906, the Princely Sailors' Association of Schaumburg-Lippe (from 1937 on, Schaumburg-Lippischer Seglerverein, SLSV) in 1908. They were the forerunners of numerous sailing clubs to be founded in subsequent decades. Very soon, nationally and internationally important regattas were organized on the lake. Tourism at the northern shore also developed around that time. Hikers who belonged to the "Wandervogel" movement and other pioneers searching for "pristine nature" landed at the White Mountain. Other visitors followed soon. With the outbreak of the First World War, visitor numbers declined dramatically, and some of the establishments did not survive the war.

Das 1899 erbaute Strandhotel war für Steinhuder Verhältnisse geradezu mondän und Motiv zahlreicher Ansichtskarten
The beach hotel, built in 1899, was almost glamorous for Steinhude standards. Its picture can still be seen on numerous postcards

Das Steinhuder Strandbad in den 1950er Jahren
The Steinhude bathing beach in the 1950s

Rechts: Um 1900 wurde das Steinhuder Meer auch als Segelrevier entdeckt. Sichtbar stolz präsentieren sich diese Segler
Right: Around 1900, Lake Steinhude was also discovered as a sailing area. It is obvious how proud these sailors were

Ihm zum Opfer fiel auch ein gigantisches Freizeit- und Ferienprojekt des hannoverschen Keksfabrikanten Hermann Bahlsen, der vor 1914 einen zwei Kilometer langen Norduferstreifen gekauft hatte, um dort Hotels, Restaurants, Bootshäuser, eine Badeanstalt und mehr zu errichten. Lediglich der Steinhuder-Meer-Bahn und den Landwirten an ihrer Strecke bescherte der Hamstertourismus infolge der Lebensmittelnot in der zweiten Kriegshälfte gute Geschäfte.

One of its victims included a giant leisure and vacation project planned by biscuit manufacturer Hermann Bahlsen from Hannover, who purchased a two kilometres' long stretch on the northern shore earmarked for hotels, restaurants, boat houses, swimming baths and more. Only the Lake Steinhude Railway and the farmers situated along its route recorded good business thanks to wide-spread "Hamstertourismus" (hoarding tourism) when food became scarce in the second half of the war. After the First World War, the efforts were intensified. Bathing, rowing, sailing and other recreational

Links: Das zugefrorene Meer ließ sich auch mit Fahrrädern überqueren – erstmals 1890, Jahrzehnte, bevor diese Aufnahme entstand
Left: It was possible to cross the frozen lake by bike – ventured for the first time in 1890, which was decades before this picture was taken

Rechts: Die Söhne des Keksfabrikanten Hermann Bahlsen mit dessen Architekten Karl Siebrecht
Right: The sons of biscuit manufacturer Hermann Bahlsen with his architect Karl Siebrecht

Ein Zeppelin über dem Steinhuder Meer, um 1930
A Zeppelin airship above Lake Steinhude, around 1930

Nach dem Ersten Weltkrieg ging es mit verdoppelter Intensität weiter. Baden, Rudern, Segeln und andere Wasservergnügen wurden zum Volkssport, und das Steinhuder Meer wurde für ein wachsendes Einzugsgebiet zum Ziel regelmäßiger Wochenendausflüge. In Steinhude, Großenheidorn und Mardorf sprossen erste Wochenendhauskolonien aus dem Boden. Die beiden Südufergemeinden eröffneten Strandbäder, während sich am Nordufer um den Weißen Berg ein „wilder" Badetourismus entwickelte. Um Steinhude für breitere Bevölkerungskreise noch attraktiver zu machen, wurde mithilfe des nationalsozialistischen Reichsarbeitsdienstes ein dem Ortskern vorgelagerter künstlicher Damm angelegt. Dieser diente als Basis für eine Uferpromenade, auf der es sich herrlich flanieren ließ. Zwar kamen auch immer mehr Besucher mit dem PKW an den See, aber insbesondere durch die StMB wurde das Steinhuder Meer für die Bewohner der nahen Großstadt an der Leine zum „Wannsee von Hannover" oder zu „Hannovers Adria". Die Bahn spülte vor allem sonntags Tausende von Ausflüglern in den Flecken, die Wege zum und am Meer waren „schwarz vor Menschen", wie es in zeitgenössischen Berichten und Erinnerungen heißt.

water activities became popular sports, and Lake Steinhude turned into an increasingly popular destination for weekend excursions. In Steinhude, Großenheidorn and Mardorf, the first few weekend home colonies mushroomed. The two municipalities on the southern shore opened bathing beaches, while "wild" bathing tourism developed on the northern shore. In order to make Steinhude even more attractive for the wider public, an artificial embankment was constructed in front of the town centre with the help of the National Socialist Reich Labour Service. It served as the basis for a waterfront promenade designed for leisurely walks. Even though more and more visitors came by car, it was mainly thanks to the StMB that Lake Steinhude became the "Wannsee of Hannover" or "Hannover's Adriatic Sea" for the inhabitants of the nearby major city. Especially on Sundays, the railway brought thousands of excursionists to the market town, and we know from reports and memories from the time that the paths leading to and from the Lake were "black with people".

Badevergnügen in den 1920er Jahren
Bathing fun in the 1920s

Erst nach dem Bau der Promenade Ende der 1930er Jahre war ein Uferspaziergang in Steinhude möglich
Walking along the shore in Steinhude only became possible after the construction of the promenade in the 1930s

Auswanderer am „Ratskellersteg" in Steinhude, vor dem Bau der Promenade. Im Hintergrund ist die Seegerssche Lederfabrik sichtbar
Auswanderer boats at the "Ratskellersteg" in Steinhude, before the promenade was built. The Seeger leather factory can be seen in the background

Bald nach dem Ende des Zweiten Weltkriegs setzte sich diese Entwicklung fort. Vor allem das bewaldete und wenig bebaute Nordufer wurde in den 1950er und 1960er Jahren von Freizeitbewohnern kolonisiert. Zeltplätze und Campingflächen wuchsen in der Presse zum „größten Campingplatz Norddeutschlands", und 1967 zählte man hier bereits 450 Wochenendhäuser. Auf einer Länge von 3,5 Kilometern wurde das Schilf entfernt und ein 25 Meter breiter Sandstrand aufgeschüttet. Immer mehr Stege reihten sich vor allem hier und in Steinhude aneinander, um Liegeplätze für die bald 6000 Segelboote bereitzustellen.

Die große Attraktivität des Steinhuder Meeres drohte ihm zum Verhängnis zu werden, zumal auch die Landwirtschaft, die Torfgewinnung und zwei Kläranlagen, die ihre Abwässer in den See leiteten, das natürliche Gleichgewicht des Meeres und seiner Uferregionen bedrohten.

Durch die Ausweisung mehrerer Naturschutzgebiete, die Deklarierung des Meeres zum „Feuchtgebiet internationaler Bedeutung" gemäß Ramsar-Konvention (in der iranischen Stadt Ramsar 1971 verabschiedetes internationales Schutzabkommen) und die Gründung des Naturparks „Steinhuder Meer" wird seit den 1960er Jahren den Gefährdungen des Meeres entgegengesteuert. Träger des Naturparks ist die Region Hannover, die mit den angrenzenden Landkreisen Schaumburg und Nienburg Vereinbarungen getroffen hat.

Links: Einen schönen Überblick über Steinhude zeigt diese Luftaufnahme aus den 1950er Jahren. Das Bild beherrschen die frühere Lederfabrik, die Uferpromenade und der Ratskellersteg
Left: This aerial photograph from the 1950s shows a beautiful view over Steinhude. The picture is dominated by the old leather factory, the promenade and the landing bridge at the town hall cellar

were counted here. Over a stretch of 3.5 kilometres, water reeds were removed and a 25 metres' wide beach was created. Here and in Steinhude, more and more landing stages were built to provide moorages for almost 6000 sailing boats. The great attractiveness of Lake Steinhude threatened to become its doom, especially as agriculture, peat production and two sewage plants, which directed their waste waters into the lake, also posed a further threat to the natural balance of the lake and its shore regions.

Diverse measures have been implemented since the 1960s to counter the threats the lake was facing, among these the protection of several landscapes, the declaration of the lake as a "Wetland of International Importance" according to the Ramsar Convention (an international treaty on nature conservation agreed in the Iranian town of Ramsar in 1971) and the foundation of the "Lake Steinhude" Nature Reserve. The Hannover Region is the sponsor of the nature reserve. It has signed agreements with the bordering districts of Schaumburg and Nienburg.

This development continued soon after the end of the Second World War. In the 1950s and 1960s, leisure time residents colonized in particular the wooded and little developed northern shore. Tent pitches and camping grounds mushroomed into what the press called the "biggest camping site in Northern Germany", and in 1967, already 450 weekend homes

Unten: Ansichtskarte aus den 1920er Jahren vom „Steenewark" (Steinwerk, also ein befestigtes Uferstück)
Bottom: Postcards from the 1920s showing the "Steenewark" (stonework, meaning a paved stretch of shore)

Die erfolgreiche Arbeit des Naturparks wird belegt durch mehrere Auszeichnungen beim Wettbewerb der Naturparke. Förderlich für das Steinhuder Meer ist auch, dass das frühere Gegeneinander der Anrainer-Kommunen einem konstruktiven Miteinander gewichen ist. So haben sich die Städte Neustadt a. Rbge. und Wunstorf zusammengeschlossen, um ein „Integriertes Ländliches Entwicklungskonzept" (ILEK) für das Gebiet Steinhuder Meer/ Unteres Leinetal zu erarbeiten. Eines der Ziele ist es, die Attraktivität des Steinhuder Meeres zu bewahren bzw. zu steigern; der Erhalt des Meeres selbst und ein damit verbundener ausreichend hoher Wasserstand wird dazu als „essentiell" angesehen. Weitere Instrumente zur Erreichung des Zieles sind die Schaffung von Schlechtwetterangeboten, die Verbesserung des Wegenetzes und die Förderung von Aktivtourismus, etwa durch das Angebot von Themenrouten. Man sieht: Die Entwicklung am Steinhuder Meer bleibt spannend!

The successful work of the Nature Reserve has been proven by several awards it received at the competition of nature reserves. Lake Steinhude also benefits from the fact that the competition of riparian municipalities has been replaced by a constructive cooperation. For example, the towns of Neustadt a. Rbge. and Wunstorf have joined forces to develop an "Integrated Rural Development

Ein Familienidyll am Nordufer, 1950er Jahre
An idyllic family gathering on the northern shore, around the 1950s

Concept" (Integriertes Ländliches Entwicklungskonzept; ILEK) for the Lake Steinhude/Lower Leine River region. One of its goals is to preserve and increase the attractiveness of Lake Steinhude; against this background, the preservation of the lake itself and, in this connection, adequately high water levels are considered "essential" prerequisites. Other instruments aimed at achieving this goal include the creation of bad weather offers, the improvement of the road network, and the promotion of active tourism, for example by offering themed routes. You see: Development at Lake Steinhude remains an exciting topic!

Ein anderes Familienidyll, 50 Jahre früher, in den „Lüttjen Deilen", Wiesenstücken vor dem Strandhotel. Hier entwickelte sich die erste Wochenendhauskolonie

Another idyllic family gathering, 50 years earlier, on the lawns in front of the beach hotel, called the "Lüttjen Deilen". The first weekend home colony was built here

Wilhelmstein

Text: Bodo Dringenberg und Klaus Fesche

Der Stein, der Schaumburg-Lippe rettete

The rock that saved Schaumburg-Lippe

Im Jahr 1790

Mit einem Wilhelmstein kann man niemandem auflauern, kein Land erobern. Er ist so etwas wie die steingewordene Defensive. Graf Wilhelm war Theoretiker und Verfechter des Defensivkrieges gewesen, nur dieser Krieg zur reinen Selbstverteidigung erschien ihm rechtmäßig zu sein. Und defensiver als der Wilhelmstein lässt sich nun wirklich keine Festung denken.

~

In the year 1790

With a Wilhelmstein, you cannot waylay anybody, you cannot conquer land. It is something like a rock-hewn defence. Count Wilhelm was a theoretician and a convinced advocate of defensive war; he strongly believed that only a war purely aimed at self-defence was justified. And one cannot imagine a fortress more defensive than Wilhelmstein.

~

Ein Jahrtausende alter Einbaum und eine Kanone aus dem 18. Jahrhundert auf dem Dachboden des Schlösschens auf dem Wilhelmstein
A several thousand years old dugout canoe and a cannon from the 18th century are exhibited in the attic of the little castle on Wilhelmstein

7. Januar 1790. Diese Nacht ist grausam. Böen, schwerer, eisiger Regen – ein teuflisches Treiben, ein Wetter wie aus einem Guss. Aber trefflich für ihn und sein Vorhaben. Er blickt sich um. Hier draußen auf dem Wilhelmstein ist sonst keiner, will keiner sein. Die Festungswache hockt außer Sicht im Eingangsgewölbe der Sternschanze.
In den Baracken der Außenwerke liegen die wachfreien Soldaten auf ihren Pritschen, einige essen noch heißen Grützbrei mit Käse oder Erbsenkost, andere würfeln bei warmem, dünnem Bier. Alle suchen sich vor dieser besonders unwirtlichen Inselnacht zu schützen ...

~

7th January 1790. This night is truly dreadful. Strong gusts, heavy, icy rain – a torrential downpour from hell. However, perfect for his plan. He is looking around. Out here on Wilhelmstein, there is no one else, no one wishes to be here. The fortress guard is cowering out of sight in the vault at the entrance to the star-shaped entrenchment. In the barracks of the barbicans, the soldiers who are not on guard are lying on their beds, some still busy eating grits with cheese or peas, others throwing dice while drinking thin warm beer. Everybody is trying to protect himself from this particularly inhospitable night on the island ...

~

Seite zuvor: unter dem friedlichen Grün sind die Reste der militärischen Anlage aus dem 18. Jahrhundert noch gut zu erkennen, beherrscht von der Sternschanze in der Mitte
Previous page: Underneath the peaceful green, the remnants of the military structure from the 18th century can still be seen, dominated by the star-shaped entrenchment in the centre

Auch mit dem Wilhelmstein als Motiv wurden zahlreiche Ansichtskarten gedruckt, insbesondere als er noch die Hauptattraktion des Steinhuder Meeres war
Wilhelmstein fortress was printed on numerous postcards, especially when it was still the main attraction of Lake Steinhude

Was Mammwah sah hinter einigen kleinen Häuschen auf winzigen Inseln, das kannte er, das war eine gewöhnliche symmetrische Sternschanze. Die hieß einfach so, weil sie auf den Plänen und Karten wie ein stumpfzackiger viereckiger Stern aussieht. Aus Mammwahs Perspektive war der Wilhelmstein zunächst nichts als ein auffallend kleines Bauwerk gewesen, das zwar drohend aus dem Binnenmeer hervorragte, aber zugleich ein wenig verloren auf dem Wasserspiegel wirkte. Eigentlich eine simple kleine symmetrische Landfestung, dachte er, bloß der Wassergraben drum herum ist riesig und asymmetrisch, das einzig Große am Wilhelmstein.

Mammwah knew what he saw behind some small houses on tiny islands: it was an ordinary symmetrical star-shaped entrenchment. The origin of the name is obvious, as it looks like a rectangle star with blunt points on plans and maps. From Mammwah's perspective, Wilhelmstein initially seemed to be nothing but a striking little building, that even though towering menacingly out of the inland lake, also looked a little lost on the water surface. It's actually a small and simple symmetrical land fortress, he thought, just the moat surrounding seems giant and asymmetrical, the only big part of Wilhelmstein.

Vom Steinhuder Ufer ist der Wilhelmstein etwa drei Kilometer entfernt
Wilhelmstein fortress is situated approximately three kilometres off shore at Steinhude

*Während der Dunkelheit wurden die Gefangenen in zwei nicht mehr benötigte Kasematten-Räume eingesperrt. Sie hatten keine eigene Feuerung, nur etwas Tageslicht drang indirekt durch naheliegende Schießscharten und die Luft war dumpf und stickig. Immerhin bekamen die Gefangenen, wenn sie nicht kurzzeitig zu verschärftem Arrest bei Wasser und Brot verurteilt waren, die normalen Rationen der Soldaten. Außerdem konnten sie zur Arbeit regelmäßig ihre klammen Verließe verlassen. Vor sich hinsiechende Gefangene wollte man auf gar keinen Fall hier in der Festung heranzüchten. Es galt, die Gefährdung der Kampfmoral, besonders aber Ansteckungen zu vermeiden. Einige Insassen mussten in einer der leeren, im Obergeschoß befindlichen Offiziersstuben bestimmte Dinge herstellen, wozu die Anfertigung von Feuerlöscheimern gehörte und das Spinnen von Garn.
Die meisten Gefangenen besserten das unaufhörlich von Wasser, Wind und Eis demolierte Inselufer aus. Einige kümmerten sich um*

Mörser und Kanonenkugeln in den Kasematten der Sternschanze
Mortars and cannonballs in the casemates of the star-shaped embankment

*die Pflege der 16 winzigen Gärten auf den Bastionen, Courtinen und Ravelins, die nach 1787 für Gemüse und Kräuter angelegt worden waren.
Aber alle mussten zu schwerster Plackerei ran, wenn es galt, im Winter das bedrohlich wachsende und herantreibende Eis aufzuhauen ...*

When it was dark, the prisoners were locked up in two redundant casemate rooms. No fire was lit there, only a little indirect daylight came through the nearby embrasures. The air was stale and stuffy. At least the prisoners received the normal food rations allotted to the soldiers, unless they were sentenced to detention with only water and bread.
They could leave their humid dungeons regularly for work. Ailing prisoners was the last thing they needed here in the fortress. Demoralization, but particularly infections, were to be avoided at all cost. Some of the inmates had to produce certain objects in the empty officers' billets on the top level, for example water buckets required for fire extinguishing, and yarn. Most of the prisoners were continuously busy repairing the island shore, which was incessantly damaged by water, wind and ice. Some tended to the 16 tiny gardens on the bastions, curtain walls and ravelins, which were created for growing vegetables and herbs after 1787.
In winter, though, everybody had to join in and work like slaves to hack the menacingly growing, floating ice ...

Luftbild vom Wilhelmstein aus den 1930er Jahren
Aerial photograph of Wilhelmstein from the 1930s

Seit einigen Jahren präsentiert der Verein „Meerkunstraum" auf dem Wilhelmstein Kunst in Glashäusern
For a few years now, the "Meerkunstraum" association exhibits art in glass houses on Wilhelmstein

So wie im vorangegangenen Romantextauszug stellt sich dessen Autor Bodo Dringenberg das Leben und die Atmosphäre auf dem Wilhelmstein vor.

Graf Wilhelm reagierte mit dem Bau der Fortifkation auf die Erfahrungen des Siebenjährigen Krieges und des Einfalls der französischen Armee in Norddeutschland. Diese hatte auch schaumburg-lippische Dörfer und Flecken in Mitleidenschaft gezogen, was den Grafen, der den Franzosen 1759 in der Schlacht bei Minden selbst als Artillerie-Befehlshaber der deutsch-britischen Koalitionsarmee begegnet war, zum Nachdenken über die Verteidigung seines Landes bewogen haben mag. Dabei dachte er aber nicht nur an Frankreich oder andere auswärtige Großmächte, auch durch deutsche Nachbarstaaten war die Eroberung Schaumburg-Lippes zu befürchten, wie sich zehn Jahre nach Graf Wilhelms Tod zeigen sollte – doch dazu später.

This text is an excerpt from a novel written by Bodo Dringenberg and describes how the author imagined life and atmosphere on Wilhelmstein fortress.

It was the experience from the Seven Years' War and the invasion of Northern Germany by the French Army that made Count Wilhelm build the fortification. The villages and market towns of Schaumburg-Lippe also suffered during these wars, which might have made the Count think about the defence of his land, as he had had encounters with the French in the battle near Minden in 1759. However, it is likely that not only France or other major foreign powers were on his mind – German neighbouring states also posed the threat of possibly trying to conquer the Principality of Schaumburg-Lippe, which, eventually, turned out to be true – but more about this further on.

Dass der Wilhelmstein auch ein beliebtes Ziel von Segeltouren ist, zeigt diese Ansichtskarte um 1930
As can be seen on this picture postcard, taken around 1930, Wilhelmstein fortress was also a popular destination for sailing tours

Kurz vor Sonnenuntergang ist die Stimmung auf dem Wilhelmstein am schönsten
The atmosphere on Wilhelmstein fortress is most beautiful just before sunset

Im Kopf des Landesfürsten reifte also die Idee, eine Verteidigungsfestung zu errichten, die unangreifbar wäre, wenn sie im Steinhuder Meer errichtet würde. Ein kühner Gedanke, ein schwieriges Projekt – doch Wilhelm gelang seine Realisierung, in dem er die Meeranwohner in jahrelangen Transporten und Arbeiten eine künstliche Insel aufschütten ließ, auf der anschließend eine moderne, mit Kanonen übersäte Festung errichtet wurde. Die zur Arbeit herangezogenen Bauern und Fischer taten dies nicht immer ohne Widerstand, und den Steinhudern brummte der Graf einmal eine saftige Geldstrafe auf, nachdem sie gestreikt hatten.

Thus, the idea of erecting a defence fortress developed in the sovereign's head – a fortress that would be impossible to attack if constructed in Lake Steinhude. A bold thought and a difficult project – but Wilhelm carried it out successfully. For years, he required the residents to transport sand and stones to build an artificial island on which then a modern fortress was erected, strewn with cannons. The farmers and fishermen forced to carry out the work did so not without resistance, and on one occasion the count imposed a heavy fine on the Steinhude population after they had gone on strike.

Die Wehrhaftigkeit des Wilhelmsteins resultiert – außer aus seiner Lage im Meer – aus der starken Bewaffnung ebenso wie aus seinen undurchdringlichen Mauern, in die wiederum zahlreiche Schießscharten eingelassen sind. Die Inschrift bezieht sich auf den Bau der Festung; das Aufschütten der Insel begann schon 1761
Apart from its situation in the lake, the good fortification of Wilhelmstein fortress was ensured by heavy weapons and its impenetrable walls provided with a large number of embrasures. The inscription refers to the construction of the fortress; raising the island began as early as 1761

Im Jahre 1767 war die Verteidigungsanlage schließlich fertiggestellt, und neben ihrer Besatzung zog dort noch eine Militärschule ein, deren berühmtester Schüler der spätere preußische Heeresreformer Scharnhorst war. Auf der Schule wurden nicht nur Strategie und Taktik unterrichtet, sondern auch Fächer wie Landwirtschaft, Geographie oder Mathematik. Zudem wurden hier neue Waffensysteme entwickelt, vor allem der „Steinhuder Hecht", ein U-Boot, das Wilhelms Ingenieur-Offizier Praetorius entworfen hatte.

Nach seinen Plänen wurde der Hecht auch gebaut und eine Weile als Modell in den schaumburg-lippischen Flottenlisten geführt; für einen wirklich einsatzfähigen Prototypen kam die Erfindung jedoch Hundert Jahre zu früh.

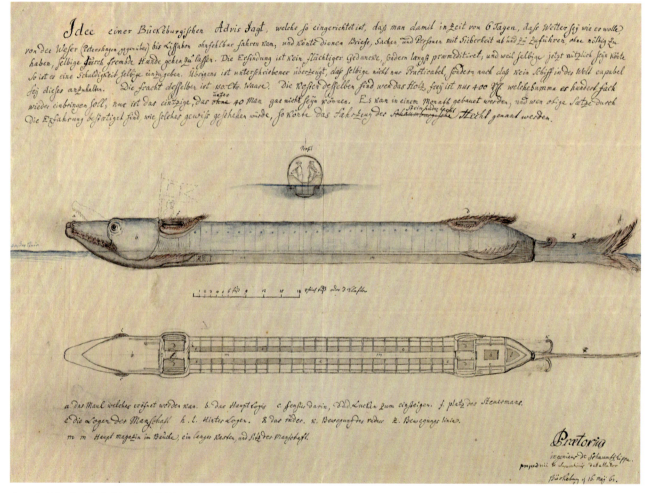

Der „Steinhuder Hecht" in einer Zeichnung seines Konstrukteurs Praetorius
The "Steinhuder Hecht" ("Steinhude Pickerel") drawn by its designer Praetorius

Bootshaus auf dem Wilhelmstein
Boat house on Wilhelmstein fortress

Finally, in 1767, the defence structure was completed, and besides its staff, a military academy moved in. Its most famous student was no other than Scharnhorst, who was later to become the reformer of the Prussian army. The academy's curriculum not only covered strategy and tactics, but also included subjects such as agriculture, geography or mathematics. In addition, new weapon systems were developed here, of which the "Steinhuder Hecht" ("Steinhude Pickerel") is especially worth mentioning: a submarine designed by Wilhelm's engineer and officer Praetorius.

The "Hecht" was built according to his plans and, for a while, was kept as a model on the lists of the Schaumburg-Lippe fleet; unfortunately, it was invented hundred years too early to become a truly usable prototype.

Im Jahre 1787 kam es schließlich zur – einzigen – militärischen Bewährungsprobe des Wilhelmsteins. Im Februar des Jahres verschied Graf Philipp Ernst, der Nachfolger Graf Wilhelms, der seinerseits zehn Jahre zuvor gestorben war. Nun sah der Landgraf von Hessen-Kassel die Gelegenheit, das kleine Schaumburg-Lippe zu annektieren, und ließ die gesamte Grafschaft von seinen Truppen besetzen. Nur der Wilhelmstein als letzte Bastion schaumburg-lippischer Souveränität ließ sich nicht erobern – Graf Wilhelms Projekt erwies sich als bestens durchdacht und verwirklicht. Nach zwei Monaten sahen sich die Hessen gezwungen, die Belagerung der Inselfestung abzubrechen, denn am kaiserlichen Hof in Wien war entschieden worden, dass die hessische Landnahme unrecht sei.

Die Legende, dass der inzwischen in hannoverschen Diensten stehende Scharnhorst durch nächtliche Versorgungslieferungen seinen einstigen Kameraden auf dem Wilhelmstein geholfen habe, lässt sich nicht durch Belege ins Reich der Fakten überführen.

Aber der Wilhelmstein wurde deutschlandweit zum Mythos, und bald begann ein jährlich ansteigender Strom von Neugierigen, die sich für die „uneinnehmbare" Inselfestung interessierten – der Keim des Steinhuder-Meer-Tourismus war gelegt. Die Steinhuder, die einst auf Kriegsfuß mit ihrem Landesherrn gestanden hatten, ehrten ihn 200 Jahre später nicht ohne Grund mit der Benennung ihrer „Graf-Wilhelm-Schule" und der „Graf-Wilhelm-Straße": Statt Steinen und anderem Baumaterial bringen sie heute gegen gutes Geld jährlich Zehntausende Touristen auf den Wilhelmstein.

In 1787, Wilhelmstein fortress had to pass its – only – military test. In February of that year, Count Philipp Ernst had died. He had been Count Wilhelm's successor, who had died ten years earlier. The Landgrave of Hesse-Kassel decided to seize the opportunity and annex the small Principality of Schaumburg-Lippe. His troops occupied the entire principality. Only Wilhelmstein fortress, as the last bastion of Schaumburg-Lippe's sovereignty, could not be conquered – Count Wilhelm's project thus proved to be brilliantly conceived and implemented. After two months, the invaders from Hesse were forced to end their siege of the island fortress, as the Imperial Court in Vienna had decided that the taking of the land by Hesse was illegal.

There are, however, no records to prove the legend that Scharnhorst, who was in the services of Hannover then, had helped his former comrades on Wilhelmstein fortress by bringing them supplies at night.

Wilhelmstein fortress, however, became a myth throughout Germany, and soon saw a growing stream of curious visitors interested in the "impregnable" island fortress – which marked the beginnings of tourism at Lake Steinhude. It was thus not without reason that the Steinhude population, once at daggers drawn with their sovereign, honoured him 200 years later by naming a school "Graf-Wilhelm-Schule" and a street "Graf-Wilhelm-Straße": These days, instead of stones and other building material, they transport tens of thousands of tourists to Wilhelmstein fortress year after year – and earn good money with it.

Nach erfolgreichem Transport von Ausflüglern auf die Insel schmeckt den Berufsseglern erst einmal ein kühles Bier in geselliger Runde – egal in welchem Jahrzehnt!
After successfully transporting excursionists to the island, professional sailors enjoy a cool beer in friendly company – no matter in which decade!

Meer Handwerk

Crafts at the lake

Bootsbau

Boat building

Text: Matthias Beilken

Heute riecht es leider nur noch selten nach Holz – auf Werften, die Boote und Yachten neu bauen. In Steinhude ist das jedoch noch so. Zumindest in der Bootsweft Bopp & Dietrich im Fischerweg am Meer. Hier fliegen noch Hobelspäne, es sägen und beitelnd Bootsbaugesellen und Lehrlinge mit Holzhämmern an millimetergenau eingepassten Leisten und Decksbalken herum. Sie schwärmen wie Arbeiterameisen um noch unfertige Holzrümpfe herum, die in der Werkstatt auf Dielenboden stehen, anstatt Formteile aus Kunststoffschablonen zu frickeln - es würde dann in der Werkstatt hauptsächlich nach Styrol, dem Hauptlösungsmittel von Kunststoffen, riechen, statt nach edlem Holz.
Die Handwerker im Fischerweg betreiben nicht „l'art pour l'art". Sie pflegen nicht traditionellen Bootsbau allein seines Erhalts wegen. Denn immerhin stehen die Bootsbauer im internationalen Wettbewerb. Unter ihren Händen entstehen einige der feinsten und ausgetüfteltsten Rennboote Europas, meist Jollenkreuzer. Und obwohl es auf der Werft nach Holz riecht, muss sich niemand einbilden, dass strickpullibewehrte Graubärte wie vor Jahrhunderten Lärchenplanken mit Kupfernieten auf Eichenspanten nageln. Moderner Holzbootsbau á la Bopp und Dietrich ist längst eine Sache von dünnen Furnierschichten, die per Vakuum unter dem

Today, unfortunately, the smell of wood has become quite rare on shipyards where new boats and yachts are built. In Steinhude, however, you can still smell it. At least at Bopp & Dietrich shipyard in the street Fischerweg by the lake. Here, wood shavings are still flying, experienced boat building craftsmen and apprentices are sawing and chiselling with mallets on frames and deck beams, fitted accurately to the millimetre. Like worker ants, they swarm around unfinished wooden hulls mounted on the wooden floor in the workshop, rather than carving mouldings out of plastic stencils – in that case the workshop would mostly smell of styrene, the main solvent used in plastics, and not wood. But the craftsmen in the street Fischerweg by the lake do not just do their work for the mere sake of keeping traditional boat building alive. After all, boat builders also face international competition. Some of the finest and most sophisticated speedboats in Europe, mostly dinghy cruisers, have been built by their hands. And even though it smells of wood at this shipyard, one should not make the mistake and imagine some grey-bearded men in knitted jerseys who spend their days mounting larch planks with copper rivets on oak frames. Today, modern wooden boat building "Bopp and Dietrich style" works with thin veneer layers that are bent into precisely calculated shapes using a vacuum press and high-performance synthetic resin.

Einsatz von Hochleistungskunstharz in eine exakt berechnete Form gebogen werden. Doch die Furnierstreifen bestehen eben aus Holz. Und Holz muss eben nach wie vor gesägt, gebeitelt, geschliffen und lackiert werden. Daher zählt die Werft streng genommen zu den Traditionsbetrieben der Bootsmanufakturen, von denen es in ganz Europa nur noch wenige gibt.

Der Betrieb entstand Mitte der 80er Jahre aus einem Abzweiger einer anderen Steinhuder Werft (die nicht mehr existiert) und etablierte sich in Windeseile als Spezialmanufaktur für Rennboote aus Holz. Aber auch große Yachten verließen die Werft, so die 42 Fuß große (Segler messen immer in Fuß!) Fahrtenyacht „Milonga" des Akademischen Segelvereins zu Hannover, die seitdem über viele Ozeane getörnt ist. Freilich mussten vor der Auslieferung ein paar Ziegel aus der Hallentorwand gebrochen werden: Normalerweise verlassen eben wesentlich kleinere Boote die Werft. Aber selbst die große „Milonga" war eine – wen überrascht's – lupenreine und saubere Holzyacht.

Kein Wunder also, dass eine Werft wie Bopp & Dietrich reihenweise Bundessieger im jährlichen Bootsbauer-Contest produziert. Und dass die Regatta-Ranglisten ehemals gespickt von Booten waren, die aus Steinhuder Produktion kamen. Jollenkreuzer, Zugvögel, Piraten, O-Jollen ... alles vom feinsten. Der Prototyp des Zugvogels – die berühmte Nummer Eins von 1963 – kam zwar ursprünglich nicht vom Steinhuder Meer, wurde dort aber jahrzehntelang kompetent gewartet.

Denn die Meer-Region ist stärker in Werfttradition verwurzelt, als gemeinhin angenommen wird. Eine Tradition, die bis in die Mitte des 18. Jahrhunderts zurückgeht und auf das Militär und der Festung Wilhelmstein gründet. Schon damals entstanden abenteuerliche Konstruktionen, die vor dem Hintergrund der Zeit wohl als sehr avantgardistisch und innovativ gelten mussten – heute als ausgesprochen spleenig. Beispielsweise das Tauchboot „Steinhuder Hecht",

Seite zuvor: Zu „Vorne" sagt man Bug: Ein Rumpf entsteht
Previous page: The front of a ship is called the bow. A hull is made

Exakt: Holzleisten werden millimetergenau eingepasst
Precision: Wooden frames are fitted accurately to the millimetre

Tradition: Hier fliegen noch Hobelspäne
Tradition: Here, wood shavings are still flying

The veneer strips, though, are made of wood. And wood still needs to be sawed, chiselled, sanded and painted. Strictly speaking, the shipyard therefore counts among the traditional boat manufactures, of which there are only a few left in entire Europe.

The company was established in the mid-1980s from a branch of another Steinhude shipyard (which no longer exists) and very quickly made a name for itself as specialist manufacturer of wooden speedboats. But the shipyard has also built some very large yachts, among them the 42 feet long (yachtsmen always measure in feet!) cruising yacht "Milonga" of Hannover Academic Sailing Club, which has since travelled many oceans. For its delivery, a few bricks had to be broken out of the entrance-wall, as the shipyard was designed for much smaller boats. But – no surprise here – even the big "Milonga" is a meticulously and cleanly built wooden yacht. No wonder then that a shipyard like Bopp & Dietrich has produced one winner after the other at the annual German boat builder contest. And that regatta ranking once included many boats from Steinhude production. Dinghy cruisers, "Zugvogel"-dinghies, pirate dinghies, Olympic dinghies ... only the finest of the finest. Even though the prototype of the "Zugvogel"-dinghy – the famous "Number One" from 1963 – was not originally made at Lake Steinhude, it was competently serviced here for decades.

In fact, the lake region's roots in shipyard tradition go deeper than is widely assumed. It is a tradition that dates back to the mid-18th century and that originated from the army and Wilhelmstein fortress. Even in those days, some rather daring designs were conceived that were probably considered extremely avant-garde and innovative at the time. Today, we might just call them nutty. One example is the submarine "Steinhuder Hecht" ("Steinhude Pickerel"), which had been designed in the hope of reaching Lisbon in a six days' long underwater journey.

Ende vom Bau: Alles im Lack! *The last step: paint until it shines!*

bei dessen Planung man in einer sechstägigen Tauchfahrt Lissabon zu erreichen hoffte, oder das amphibische See- und Flusspferd „Hippopotame": Eine Art Holzpferd mit Schubkarren-Appeal, das schwimmen und geschoben werden konnte. Ein krudes Gefährt mit dem man „mit Vorteil durch die ganze Welt reisen ... und dem Feinde durch Ruinierung der Magazyne und Brücken großen Schaden" zufügen konnte – angeblich (ob das Holztier jemals gebaut worden ist, wissen wir nicht). Urheber dieser ulkigen Ideen war Jakob Chrysostomus Praetorius, der ein Hofdesigner von Graf Wilhelm war. Dem es wiederum offensichtlich um Marine- und Militärangelegenheiten sehr ernst war. Denn auf dem Meer unterhielt er eine ganze, wenn auch kleine, Flotte zum Schutz der Festung Wilhelmstein. „Vier Barquen, ein Magazinschiff, ein Wachtschiff" und zwei weitere Segler. Eine der „Barquen", der „Schwan", wurde offensichtlich als Mäh- und Entschlammboot eingesetzt. An Bord: Mudde-Mühle mit Löffeln. Später war noch die Rede von drei „Falconetschiffen" (Kanonenbooten), wovon eines in einer „fischartigen Gestalt gebauet" war und somit das Tauchboot werden sollte. Teilweise hatten die Schiffe richtige Rahriggs, teils Lateinersegel und teilweise nur Riemen. Putzig, angesichts der Tatsache, dass das Steinhuder Meer im Durchschnitt lediglich 1,35 m tief und fern des Meeres ist.

Irritieren ließen sich Graf und Praetorius von solch geografischen Spitzfindigkeiten jedoch nicht. Weiter entwarfen sie possierliche – und sicherlich nach deren Meinung sehr praktische – Wasserfahrzeuge und fütterten so die Schiffbautradition am Meer. Von der Christian Dietrich mit seiner Werft im Fischerweg in Steinhude heute noch profitiert. So entwarf das Fürst-Tüftler-Duo faschinenbewehrte Behelfsflöße, um im Notfall die Festung versorgen zu können oder zerleg- und tragbare Boote, die auf diverse Eroberungszüge mitgeschleppt werden sollten. Doch, doch. Maritime Berufe waren am Steinhuder Meer schon immer „en vogue". So gab es Matrosen, die in der fürstlichen Marine dienten, Bootsbauer, Takler ... und Menschen, die sich mit Textil beschäftigten, denn die Schiffe brauchten Segel. Und die Menschen Hemden. Und der Rest sind Weber-Geschichten.

And then there was the amphibious lake and river horse "Hippopotame", which was some sort of wooden horse with the appeal of a wheelbarrow that could float and be pushed. A crude vessel supposed to offer the "benefit of travelling throughout the world ... and wreak havoc on the enemy by ruining weapon depots and bridges" – that was the idea, at least (we do not know if the wooden animal had actually ever been built). These hilarious ideas were conceived by Jakob Chrysostomus Praetorius, a designer at the court of Count Wilhelm. The latter obviously took all matters concerning the navy and the army very seriously. In fact, he maintained a complete, albeit small fleet on the lake to protect Wilhelmstein fortress. "Four barques, a magazine boat, a guard board" and two more sailing boats. One of the "barques", the "swan", was apparently used as mowing and sludge removal boat. On board: a sludge mill with spoons.

Later, there was also talk of three "falconet boats" (gunboats), one of them built in the "shape of a fish" and thus intended to be used as a submarine. Some of the boats had real square sails, others lateen sails, and others just oars. Very cute indeed, if you consider the fact that Lake Steinhude has an average depth of only 1.35 m and is situated far away from the sea.

But the Count and Praetorius were unconcerned by these geographical subtleties. They also designed some comical – and certainly, in their opinion, very practical – watercraft, feeding the shipbuilding tradition at the lake. Something that Christian Dietrich and his shipyard in Fischerweg in Steinhude benefit from to this day. The count-meets-tinkerer duo went on to design fascine-armoured makeshift rafts intended to supply the fortress in an emergency, or demountable and portable boats that were to be carried along on diverse conquering campaigns. You don't believe it? It's true. At Lake Steinhude, maritime professions have always been "en vogue". There were sailors who served in the principal navy, boat builders, riggers ... and people who worked with textiles, as the ships needed sails. And people needed shirts. And the rest are weavers' stories.

Weberei   Weaving

Text: Sabine Steuernagel

Ein Raunen ging durch den Ort, damals vor mehr als 250 Jahren. Auf einem der zahlreichen Webstühle, die in vielen Häusern klapperten, war ein ganz besonderes Kleidungsstück entstanden. Ein Hemd, das es so eigentlich nicht geben durfte. War es Handwerkskunst, Zauberei oder einfach eine perfekt geglückte Täuschung? Bis heute ist das Geheimnis um dieses einzigartige Hemd nicht gelöst. Sicher ist nur, dass das Hemd auf einem Webstuhl in Steinhude gewebt wurde. Ärmel, Schulterpasse, der lange, weiche Fall über Brust und Hüften, alles aus einem Stück. Das wohl bekannteste Zeichen für die hohe Qualität, die die Weber in Steinhude mit ihrer Arbeit erzielt hatten. Und mit dem „Hemd ohne Naht" hat der junge Webergeselle Henrich Bühmann den Steinhuder Webern ein Denkmal gesetzt.

A murmur went through the village more than 250 years ago. On one of the numerous looms that rattled along in many homes, a very special piece of clothing was created. A shirt that was actually not supposed to exist. Was it craftsmanship, magic, or simply a little luck and deception? To this day, the mystery surrounding this unique shirt has not been solved. What we do know for certain, though, is that the shirt was woven on a loom in Steinhude. Sleeves, shoulder part, the long and smooth drop over chest and hips, all from one piece. Probably the best-known symbol of the high quality that the weavers in Steinhude have achieved with their work. With the "seamless shirt", young weaver Henrich Bühmann created a monument to Steinhude weavers. What formed the place between the 18th and late 19th century, can still be experienced at the Steinhude Fisher and Weaver Muse- um. *And also at Seegers & Sohn weaving mill in Bleichenstrasse, where looms are rattling in the old factory building in Steinhude already in the ninth generation. Here, traditional and modern designs are produced for an international market. The Fisher and Weaver Museum takes visitors back in time. Dark, heavy oak furniture, small, cosy parlours, with the typical traditional wood stove called "Bollerofen", tell of the lives of fishermen and weavers who, for several generations, had lived in the house in Neuen Winkel from around 1850 to 1984.*

In den mechanischen Webereien wurden die Webmuster durch Lochkarten (links im Bild) gesteuert. Diese wurden in „Kartenschlägereien" gefertigt, zwei solcher seltenen Produktionsstätten gab es in Steinhude
In mechanical weaving mills, weaving designs were controlled by punched cards (left-sided in the picture). These were produced in "card punching shops", and two of these rare production facilities were found in Steinhude

Gebäude der Weberei Seegers & Sohn, wie es 1914 an der Bleichenstraße stand. Was aussah wie ein nicht gebrauchtes Stück Wiese wurde zur Bleiche des Leinens benötigt. Das konnte mitunter Tage dauern. Noch heute erinnert der Straßenname „Bleichenstraße" an diesen wichtigen Teil der Produktion.
The building of Seegers & Sohn weaving mill in Bleichenstrasse in 1914. What looked like an unused piece of lawn was used for bleaching linen. This could sometimes take days. To this day, the street name "Bleichenstrasse" ("Bleaching Street") reminds us of this important part of the production

Was zwischen dem 18. und ausgehenden 19. Jahrhundert den Ort prägte, ist heute nur noch im Steinhuder Fischer- und Webermuseum zu erleben. Und in der Weberei Seegers & Sohn in der Bleichenstraße, die bereits in der neunten Generation in den alten Werkshallen in Steinhude die Webstühle rattern lässt. Hier wird mit traditionellen und modernen Designs für einen internationalen Markt produziert. Das Fischer- und Webermuseum jedoch nimmt die Besucher mit in eine vergangene Zeit. Dunkle, schwere Eichenmöbel, kleine, gemütliche Stuben, mit dem typischen Bollerofen, erzählen vom Leben der Fischer und Weber, die das Haus im Neuen Winkel um 1850 bis 1984 in mehreren Generationen bewohnten. In der sogenannten „Großen Stube" steht das Schmuckstück des Hauses: ein Webstuhl aus der Zeit um 1750, der an Aktionstagen im Museum noch fachkundig bedient wird. Die Schiffchen, so wurden von den Webern die Webschützen genannt, liegen bereit, als wenn die Hausbewohner nur kurz den Webstuhl verlassen hätten. Viele Tausend Male sind damit die zu verwebenden Garne durch Kette und Schuss geführt worden. Zentimeter um Zentimeter entstand in traditioneller Handarbeit ein neues Leintuch für die Aussteuer, ein Stoffballen für den Markt in den umliegenden Städten oder ein Hemd für die Aussteuer. Und vielleicht auch, mit Anspannung und Konzentration, ein „Hemd ohne Naht". Denn es wird sich immer noch erzählt, dass in Steinhude fünf dieser wundervollen Hemden gewebt worden sein sollen. Aufgefunden wurde allerdings bis heute nur eines dieser Wunderwerke, das im Museum in Steinhude ausgestellt wird. Sicher eine spannende Frage, wo die anderen verblieben sind. Gibt es dazu noch eine geheimnisvolle Geschichte?

The gem of the house can be found in the so-called "Große Stube" ("Big Parlour"): a loom from around 1750, which is still expertly operated on special exhibition days at the museum. The shuttles, as they were called by the weavers, are lying there ready to be used as if the residents had only briefly left their loom. Many thousands of times, they were used to weave the yarns through warp and weft. Centimetre by centimetre and in traditional handicraft, a new sheet or a shirt was made for the dowry chest, or a bolt of cloth was produced for the market in nearby towns. And perhaps someone, with a lot of excitement and concentration, wove a "seamless shirt". To this day, the story goes that five of these wonderful shirts were woven in Steinhude. However, only one of these marvels has been found, which is exhibited in the museum in Steinhude. Where might the others be? Certainly an interesting question. Is there maybe another mysterious story to tell?.
Steinhude's history as a place of weavers, however, is well-documented and verified. Flax was grown on the shores of Lake Steinhude. It belongs to the bast fibres and is very difficult to manage and brittle in its natural state. The good quality of the water – it was especially "soft" as a result of the illuviation from the neighbouring swamp and the sediments accumulated on the ground – made it excellently

Stolz auf die eigene, hochwertige Arbeit. Vor der ersten Weberei der Familie Seegers von 1870 zeigte sich Friedrich Dietrich Ludolph Seegers mit seinen Arbeitern. Schon damals hatte das produzierte Leinen einen hervorragenden Ruf in Deutschland. In der sich immer weiter vergrößernden Weberei fanden viele Steinhuder Familien Arbeit
Proud of their high-quality work. Friedrich Ludolph Dietrich Seegers is pictured with his workers in front of the first weaving mill of the Seegers family in 1870. Even then, the linen produced here enjoyed an excellent reputation in Germany. Many Steinhude families found work in the continuously expanding weaving mill

Die Kastenmangel, in die „Mangelfritz" 1930 das aufgewickelte Leinen schiebt, existiert noch heute. Sie steht unter Denkmalschutz
The box-shaped mangle, into which "Mangle Fritz" feeds the rolled up linen in 1930, still exists. It is a protected heritage item

Spulengatter der Schärmaschine – zur
Vorbereitung des Webprozesses
*Creel of the warping machine – used to
prepare the weaving*

Auf einem Jaquardwebstuhl wird hochwertige
Tischwäsche hergestellt
Quality table linen is produced on a Jacquard loom

Dokumentiert und belegt jedoch ist die Geschichte Steinhudes als Ort der Weber. An den Ufern des Steinhuder Meeres wurde Flachs angebaut, der zu den Bastfasern gehört und im Urzustand eher störrisch und spröde ist. Durch die gute Qualität des Wassers – es war besonders „weich" durch die Einspülungen des benachbarten Moores und der Sedimente, die sich am Boden ablagerten – war es hervorragend zum Wässern des Flachses geeignet. Ein Prozess, der unbedingt vor dem weiteren Verarbeiten stattfinden musste. Flachs war einer der Grundstoffe, den die zahlreich am Steinhuder Meer arbeitenden Fischer zum Flicken der Netze benötigten. Da lag es nahe, den Flachs nach der Vorbehandlung zu verspinnen und nicht nur für die Netze zu verwenden. Über Jahrzehnte entstanden in Steinhude, durch viel Erfahrung und hohe Kunstfertigkeit, europaweit bekannte Leinengewebe. Tischwäsche und Aussteuerwaren wurden produziert. Diese lagen auf den großen Gütern in Schlesien und Ostpreußen genauso wie in den Wäscheschränken der weltbekannten Hotels, wie dem Adlon in Berlin.

Wer heute ans Steinhuder Meer fährt, sieht noch viele Uferbereiche, die sich fast so darstellen wie die Flachsbleichen vor Hunderten von Jahren. Wo sich heute Schilfgras im Wind wiegt, fand früher die Flachsbleiche statt. Und Straßen wie „Große Bleiche" oder „Bleichenstraße" kennzeichnen am Südufer des Meeres die frühere Bestimmung der vielen „feuchten Wiesen", wie diese Bereiche bei den Steinhudern gerne auch genannt werden. Heute stehen dort Ferienhäuser und Hotels, herrscht in den Sommermonaten fröhliches Strandleben. Früher wurde dort hart gearbeitet, um dem Meer neben dem Fisch noch ein Einkommen abzutrotzen.

suited for watering the flax. This process is vital before the flax can be used in any way. Flax was one of the raw materials that the numerous fishermen who worked at Lake Steinhude needed for mending their nets. Hence, it was obvious to spin the flax after pretreatment and to use it not only for the fishing nets. Great expertise and high craftsmanship made the linen fabric produced in Steinhude famous throughout Europe. Table linen and dowry items were among the products. These could be found on large estates in Silesia and Eastern Prussia, and also in the linen closets of world-renowned hotels such as the Adlon in Berlin. When you travel to Lake Steinhude today, you can still spot many areas on its shores that look almost like the flax bleaching grounds hundreds of years ago. In the past, flax was bleached where today reeds sway in the wind. And roads such as the "Große Bleiche" or "Bleichenstraße" on the southern shore of the lake tell of the former use of many "wet meadows", as these areas are often called among the Steinhude population. Today, there are holiday homes and hotels and happy beach life prevails during summer months. In the past, people worked very hard to wrest some income from the lake, apart from fish.

Fischerei   Fishing

Text: Klaus Fesche

Die Fischerei im Steinhuder Meer – eine lebendige Tradition
Wo ein Gewässer ist, wird auch gefischt. Schon die steinzeitlichen Einbäume, die im Steinhuder Meer oder an seinen Ufern gefunden wurden, deuten auf Fischzüge hin, die vor Tausenden von Jahren unternommen wurden. Der Fischreichtum des Sees dürfte das Motiv für die ersten Siedlungen an seinen Ufern gewesen sein. Bereits die erste Steinhude erwähnende Urkunde (1290-1300 verfertigt) betrifft die Fischer des Ortes – und ihre Pflicht, dem Bischof von Minden Fische zu liefern.

So geschätzt der Fisch an herrschaftlichen Tafeln war, so bedeutsam war er als Erwerbsgrundlage der Fischerfamilien. Das Recht, auf dem Meer zu fischen, musste jedoch von den gräflichen, später fürstlichen Behörden gepachtet werden. Die Höhe der Pacht war dabei stets umstritten, immer wieder baten die Fischer um ihre Senkung. Wohl auch, um ihre Verhandlungsposition zu stärken, gründeten sie um 1800 eine Fischereigesellschaft – Vorläuferin des noch heute bestehenden Fischereivereins Steinhude e.V. von 1928. Die Steinhuder mussten um ihre Fischereirechte immer wieder kämpfen: Schon aus dem 16. Jahrhundert sind Berichte über Konflikte mit den Mardorfern überliefert, die ihrerseits am Fischangebot des Steinhuder Meeres teilzuhaben suchten.

Fishing on Lake Steinhude – a living tradition
Where there is water, there is fishing. The dugout canoes from the Stone Age that were found in Lake Steinhude or on its shores indicate that already thousands of years ago people travelled the lake to fish. And it was probably the abundance of fish in the lake that made them settle along its shores. The first official document in which Steinhude is mentioned (dating back to 1290-1300) also refers to the fishermen of the village – and their duty to supply the Bishop of Minden with fish.

Fish was highly appreciated on the tables of sovereigns and an important source of livelihood for fishing families. The right to fish in the lake, though, had to be leased from the authorities instructed by the counts and later the ruling princes. The amount of the lease was always controversial, and fishermen repeatedly asked for a reduction. Around 1800, they formed a fishing association, probably with the aim of strengthening their bargaining position. It was the predecessor of today's Fishing Association Steinhude e.V., which was founded in 1928. Time and again, the Steinhude population had to fight for their fishing rights: Reports of conflicts with the inhabitants of Mardorf, who also wanted to have a share of the fish of Lake Steinhude, date back as far as the 16th century.

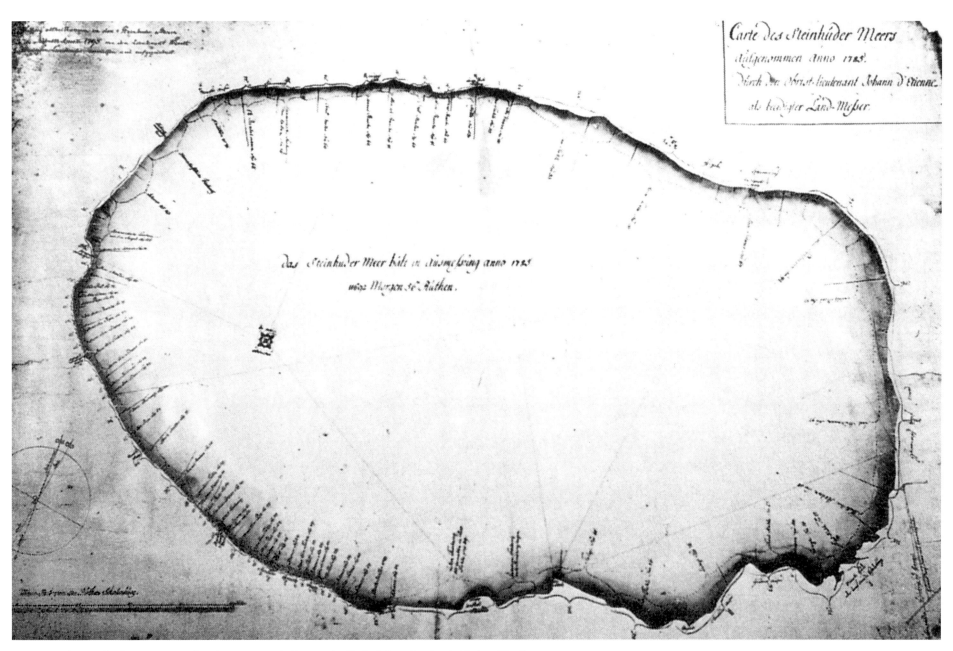

Diese Karte des Steinhuder Meeres von Oberstleutnant Jean d'Etienne zeigt die Aufteilung des Sees in Fischereidistrikte
This map of Lake Steinhude drawn by Lieutenant Colonel Jean d'Etienne shows the division of the lake into fishing districts

Ganz links: Für seine Aale ist das Steinhuder Meer berühmt
Far left: Lake Steinhude is famous for its eels

Links oben: Ein Fischer im Torfkahn prüft seine Reusen
Top left: A fisherman in his peat barge checks his fyke nets

Links unten: Blick in den Alten Winkel auf einem Foto um 1930. Fast alle Häuser auf der rechten Seite gehörten den Familien Schweer – Die übrigens nicht alle untereinander verwandt waren
Bottom left: View of the Alte Winkel on a photograph from around 1930. Almost all the houses on the right side belonged to the Schweer families – who, by the way, were not all related

Wiederholt gerieten sie mit ihnen und den Seeanwohnern aus Großenheidorn, Hagenburg und Winzlar aneinander, denen sie unberechtigtes Fischen, Fischdiebstahl oder das Zerstören von Körben vorwarfen. Immerhin konnte durchgesetzt werden, dass die Mardorfer den Fisch nur mit den Händen aus dem Meer ziehen durften. Dennoch wurde die Klage laut, dass ein Steinhuder Fischer weniger verdiene als ein Tagelöhner. Der Fischreichtum war relativ – er schwankte vor allem aus klimatischen Gründen über die Jahre, und um alle Siedlungen rund um den See zu ernähren, reichte er nicht. Spätestens im 18. Jahrhundert wurden gegen eine drohende Überfischung Regeln erlassen: Zugnetze wurden 1738 für die Laichzeit verboten, Aale durften nur montags und mittwochs gefangen werden. Ähnliche und weitere Bestimmungen durchziehen die regelmäßig erneuerten Pachtverträge.

1801 wurde das Meer in 32 Fischereidistrikte aufgeteilt, die jeweils an Fischer aus Steinhude verpachtet wurden; später kamen zuweilen auch Hagenburger oder Großenheidorner Fischer zum Zuge. Gefischt wurde mit Reusen (Körben) und Zugnetzen; die berühmten Steinhuder Aale auch mit Grundangeln – langen Leinen, an denen in bestimmten Abständen Schnüre mit Angelhaken und Ködern befestigt waren.

Um über die Runden zu kommen, mussten sich die Steinhuder Fischer so einige Tricks einfallen lassen, mit denen sie die herrschaftliche Fischereiordnung umgehen konnten. So erzählte „Janners Discher", wie er auch an Tagen, an denen nicht gefischt werden durfte, auf Beutezug gegangen war. Unter vollen Segeln fuhr er scheinbar auf dem Meer umher – was die Arbeit mit Grundangeln unmöglich gemacht hätte. Tatsächlich aber hatte er einen großen Topf hinter seinen Torfkahn gehängt, der die Fahrt so stark verlangsamte, dass die Angelleine dennoch ausgelegt werden konnte.

Das 20. Jahrhundert brachte dann zahlreiche Veränderungen

Repeatedly, they had disputes with these and the residents of other towns situated along the shores of the lake, like Großenheidorn, Hagenburg and Winzlar, accusing them of fishing without authorization, stealing fish or destroying coops. They were able to enforce that people from Mardorf were only allowed to pull the fish out of the lake with their bare hands. But there were still many complaints alleging that a fisherman in Steinhude earned less than a day labourer. The abundance of fish was relative – it fluctuated over the years, mainly due to climate, and it was not enough to feed all settlements around the lake. In the 18th century, at the latest, rules were enacted to counter the threat of overfishing: In 1738, towed nets were banned during the spawning season, and catching eels was only permitted on Mondays and Wednesdays. Regularly renewed lease contracts were full of similar and other provisions.

In 1801, the lake was divided into 32 fishing districts, which were respectively leased out to fishermen from Steinhude; later, fishermen from Hagenburg or Großenheidorn were occasionally also granted these rights. Fykes (bow nets) and towed nets were used for general fishing while the famous Steinhude eel was caught with ground fishing rods – long lines to that strings with fishing hooks and bait were attached.

To make ends meet, Steinhuder fishermen had to come up with a trick or two to bypass the strict fishing regulations imposed by the sovereign. "Janners Discher", for example, told about how he went out to catch fish even on days when fishing was banned. He travelled on the lake with full sails – which would have made working with ground fishing rods impossible. In fact, however, a big pot was trailing behind his peat barge and decelerated the speed of the boat, making it possible to cast the fishing line.

63

Auch das Netzeflicken gehört zum Fischerhandwerk – und dafür ist Feinmotorik gefragt!
Mending the nets is also part of the craft of fishing – and it requires fine motor skills!

und Neuerungen für die Fischerei im Steinhuder Meer. Zunächst, im Jahre 1900, wurde die Verpachtung neu geregelt: Ein Generalpächter, August Hübner aus Frankfurt an der Oder, pachtete die gesamte Fischerei für 12.000 Mark – gegenüber 950 Mark, die die Steinhuder Fischer bisher gezahlt hatten. Letztere wurden dann größtenteils von Hübner als Unterpächter unter Vertrag genommen. Damit sich Hübners Einsatz auch lohnte, führte er neue Bewirtschaftungs- und Fangmethoden ein. So wurden Aal- und Karpfenbrut sowie der Zander als neue Fischart im Meer ausgesetzt, zudem neue Fischereifahrzeuge in Gestalt von Angelschiffen eingeführt. Doch die Hyperinflation von 1923 versetzte dem Fischereiunternehmen Hübner einen Tiefschlag, von dem es sich nicht mehr erholte. Ab 1933 pachtete die Firma Schweer und Kuckuck die Fischerei im Steinhuder Meer.

Diese war 1919 aus dem Zusammenschluss zweier Fischhandels-Familienbetriebe entstanden, die Steinhuder Fisch überregional verkauften. Die Firma baute die von Hübner eingeführten Methoden weiter aus, setzte bis zu 100 Kilogramm Aalbrut ins Meer, ergänzte das Fischangebot um Hechte und arbeitete mit Zugnetzen von 500 bis 800 Metern Länge. 1946 fing man 1500 Zentner Fisch – das Fünffache dessen, was um 1900 aus dem See gezogen wurde.
Heute verpachtet das Land Niedersachsen die Fischereirechte am Steinhuder Meer an drei Pächter: eine Emdener Firma, den Landessportfischerverband und den Steinhuder Fischereiverein.

Ihre Traditionen feiern die Steinhuder Fischer am jährlich im Mai stattfindenden „Fischerkreidag", zu dessen Programm Torfkahnregatten, öffentliches Netzeflicken, der „Brassenschlag", mit dem „verdiente" Zugezogene zu „echten" Steinhudern erklärt werden, und natürlich Aalessen, Musik und Tanz gehören. Wichtiger Bestandteil ist auch die Ernennung eines prominenten „Freyfischers", dem daraufhin ein freier Torfstich und ein freier Fischzug zustehen. Die Steinhuder Fischereitradition ist also höchst lebendig – und wird es bleiben.

The 20th century then brought a number of changes and new regulations for fishery in Lake Steinhude. First, in 1900, the lease system was restructured: A general leaseholder, August Hübner from Frankfurt an der Oder, rented the entire fishing rights at a price of 12,000 Marks – compared to 950 Marks which Steinhude fishermen had paid previously. Most of them were then contracted by Hübner as sub-leaseholders. To make Hübner's investment worthwhile, he introduced new management and fishing practices. Eel and carp fry and perch as a new species of fish were released into the lake, and new vessels in the form of fishing boats were introduced. However, Hübner's fishing company suffered an immense blow during the hyperinflation of 1923 from which it should never recover. From 1933, the company Schweer und Kuckuck leased the fishing business in Steinhude. It had been established in 1919 from the merger of two family businesses that operated in the fishing trade and sold fish from Steinhude nationwide. The company developed the methods introduced by Hübner further, released up to 100 kilogrammes of eel fry into the lake, added pickerel to the variety of fish, and operated with 500 to 800 meters long towed nets. In 1946, 1500 hundredweights of fish were caught – five times the amount caught in the lake around 1900. Today, the State of Lower Saxony leases the fishing rights at Lake Steinhude to three leaseholders: one company from Emden, the Association of Sports Fishermen of Lower Saxony, and the Steinhude Fishery Association.

Every year in May, fishermen from Steinhude celebrate their tradition at a so-called "Fischerkreidag" fishing fair during which peat barge regattas and public net mending are organized, and also "brace batting" with that "worthy" new residents are declared "real" Steinhude inhabitants. And of course, there is eel-eating, music and dancing galore. An important part of the festivities is the appointment of a prominent "Freyfischer" (free fisherman) who then receives a free allotment of peat and a free catch of fish. Fishing tradition in Steinhude is thus very much alive – and will remain so.

Fischen am Steinhuder Meer heute
Fishing on Lake Steinhude today

Text: Heinrich K.-M. Hecht

Im Flachgebiet, in dem die Reusen liegen, lässt sich der Kahn am besten staken
The shallow waters where the fyke nets have been set up are best for punting the boat

Ein kapitaler Hecht war in der Reuse – einer von vielen an diesem Tag
A huge pickerel was in the fyke – one of many this day

Fischer's Uli …

Mittwochs ist für Ulrich Balzer „Fischtag" – er geht fischen, und da bleibt sein Laden in Neustadt am Nachmittag geschlossen.

Ich wollte einmal persönlich wissen, wie das heute von statten geht. Die Bedingungen sind suboptimal, starker Wind und Seegang. Noch bleiben wir einigermaßen trocken, da wir mit den Wellen in Richtung Ostenmeer unterwegs sind, wo Uli seine Reusen betreibt. Insgesamt sind es zur Zeit über 30 Reusen. Wir nähern uns der ersten Reuse und Uli macht den Kahn mittels einer überdimensionalen Stak-Stange, die eine eiserne Spitze besitzt, fest. Genauer: Er führt die Stange durch eine Schlinge am Boot und rammt sie dann in den moorigen Boden unter Wasser. Wollen wir hoffen, dass dieses Verfahren auch bei 6 Bft Wind noch hält!

Allerlei Fisch, den ich persönlich noch nie im Meer gesehen habe, taucht in der hochgezogenen Reuse auf. Die Fische kommen in eine mit Wasser gefüllte Tonne, und so geht es von Reuse zu Reuse weiter, bis die Stakstange unter der Last des Bootes, der Wellen und des Windes bricht! Ausgerechnet, als er gerade dabei war eine Reuse zu flicken, die von einem kapitalen Hecht an einer Sollbruchstelle zerstört war. Es bleibt an diesem Tag nicht die einzige Reuse, die geflickt werden muss. Uli bleibt ganz ruhig, nimmt sich Zeit den Schaden zu begutachten und verhindert mit einer weiteren noch intakten Stange das Treiben des Kahns, während er die Reuse flickt. Anschließend geht es zurück. Jetzt ist schöpfen angesagt, mit einem alten Eimer, denn eine Lenzvorrichtung hat der Kahn natürlich nicht. Auf der Rückfahrt haben wir leider Gegenwind und Gegenwelle. Schade eigentlich, dass ich meine Segelhose vergessen habe anzuziehen …

Uli liebt seinen Beruf. Bereits im Alter von sechs Jahren nahm ihn der Opa mit zum Angeln rund um Wunstorf und Hagenburg. Das und die Liebe zur Natur haben ihn wohl geprägt. Als gelernter Fischwirt mit Schwerpunkt Fischzucht der Seen- und Flussfischerei weiß er somit heute auch was er tut – der Fischer's Uli.

Fisher's Uli …
Wednesday is "fishing day" for Ulrich Balzer – he goes fishing and his shop in Neustadt remains closed during the afternoon.
I wanted to experience personally how it is done today. The conditions with strong winds and waves are suboptimal. But for now, we stay relatively dry as we are travelling with the waves towards the eastern section of the lake, where Uli puts out his fish traps. There are currently more than 30 fykes in total. We approach the first fyke and Uli moors the boat with an oversized iron-tipped punt pole. Or more specifically: He puts the pole through a loop on the boat and then rams it into the marshy ground under water. Let's hope this method will withstand 6 bft wind!
When the fyke is pulled up, it contains all sorts of fish, which I personally have never seen in the lake. The fish are thrown in a tub filled with water, and this process is repeated for all the other fykes until the pole breaks under the weight of the boat, the waves and the wind! Just when he was busy patching up a fyke that had been damaged by a huge pickerel at a predetermined breaking point. It will not be the only fyke that needs to be repaired this day. Uli remains calm, takes his time to inspect the damage and, using an undamaged pole, prevents the boat from drifting away while he mends the fyke. After that, we go back. Now we have to scoop out the water with an old bucket because the boat does not have a drainage device. Unfortunately, when travelling back, we have head wind and waves. Just my luck that I forgot to put on my sailing pants …
Uli loves his job. When he was just six years old, his granddad would take him along to fish around Wunstorf and Hagenburg. That and the love of nature have probably influenced him. A qualified fish farmer specialized in fish breeding in lake and river fishery, he obviously knows what he is doing today – that's Fisher's Uli.

Das Flicken der Reusen geschieht noch wie früher am einfachsten mit einer Netznadel
As in the old days, the fykes are best mended with a fishing net needle

Naturpark
Nature Reserve

Text: Thomas Brandt

Das Steinhuder Meer

Das Steinhuder Meer ist der größte See Niedersachsens. Fast 30 km² misst die Wasserfläche zwischen Mardorf im Norden und Steinhude im Süden, zwischen dem Meerbruch im Westen und dem Toten Moor im Osten. Der See ist sehr flach, die durchschnittliche Tiefe beträgt gerade einmal 1,35 m, die tiefste Stelle in den so genannten Deipen nordöstlich der Insel Wilhelmstein dürfte heute kaum mehr tiefer als 2,5 m sein.

Ein maßstabsgerechtes Modell des „Meeres" können wir schnell anfertigen. Ein dünnes DIN-A4-Blatt auf die Form des Sees zugeschnitten hätte in etwa die richtige Tiefenproportion.

Lake Steinhude

Lake Steinhude is the largest lake in Lower Saxony. The water surface measures nearly 30 km², extending from Mardorf in the north to Steinhude in the south, and from the Meerbruch conservation area in the west to the "Totes Moor" (Dead Moor) in the east. The lake is very shallow with an average depth of just 1.35 m, and the deepest point in the so-called "Deipen" north-east of Wilhelmstein is probably not deeper than 2.5 m, today.

A scale model of the lake would be easy to design. You would simply take a thin A4 sheet of paper, cut it into the shape of the lake and would get about the right depth proportion.

Zwischen dem Ostenmeer und dem Toten Moor sind heute noch Reste eines alten Kanals zu sehen. Über diesen wurde zu früheren Zeiten der Torf auf Booten aus dem Moor nach Steinhude transportiert

The remnants of an old channel are still visible between the Eastern Lake and the Dead Moor. In the past, it was used to transport peat on boats from the moor to Steinhude

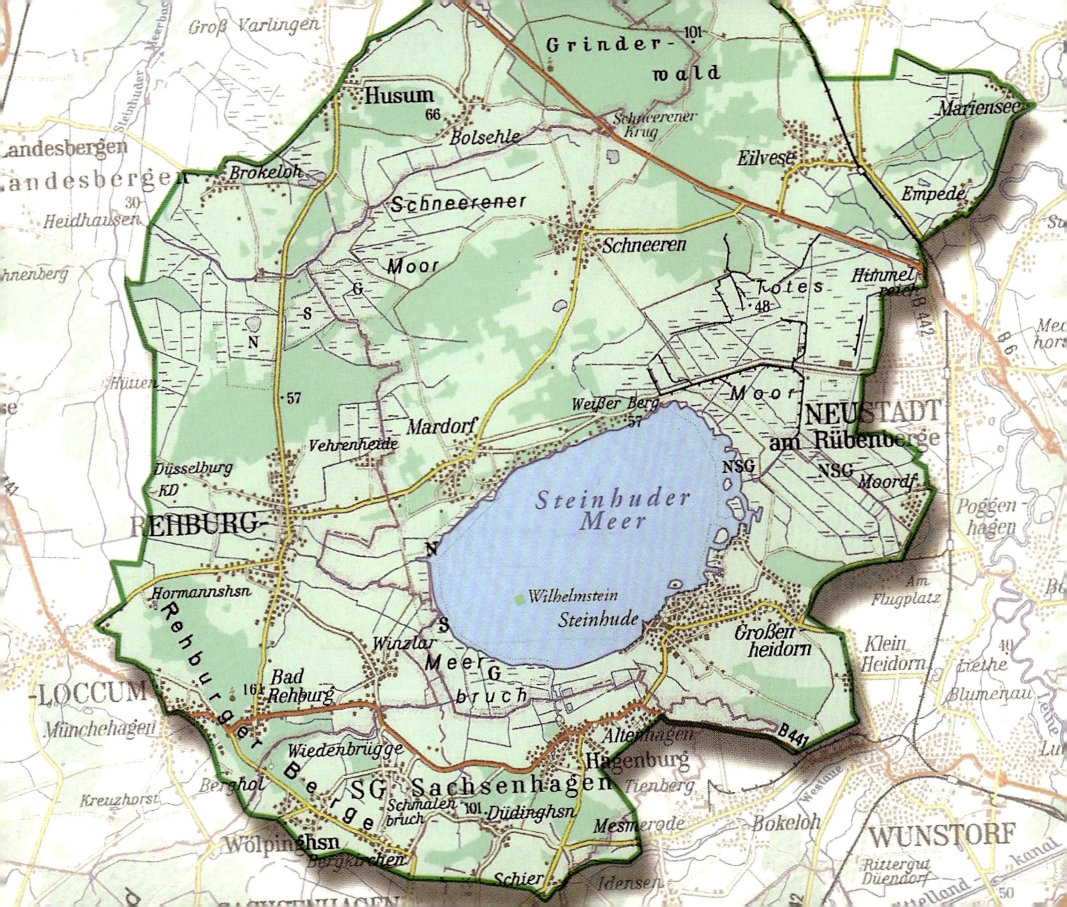

Wie das Steinhuder Meer entstand

Erdgeschichtlich gesehen ist das Steinhuder Meer ein junges Gewässer. Etwa 12.000 Jahre alt dürfte es sein, denn es entstand nach der letzten Eiszeit. Die Eisschicht reichte zwar nicht bis in unsere Region, dennoch herrschte hier Dauerfrost im Boden, wie wir ihn heute beispielsweise aus dem nördlichen Skandinavien oder Russland kennen. Als sich das Eis aus Mitteleuropa zurückzog, schmolz eine zuvor verdeckte Eislinse im Boden, das Gelände sackte ab und die Steinhuder-Meer-Senke entstand. Schließlich bliesen Winde das Becken zusätzlich aus und lagerten den Sand am Nordufer als Dünen ab. Mehr als 60 Sanddünen gibt es dort heute noch, von denen die „Weiße Düne" die mit Abstand größte ist. Von den meisten Dünen ist heute allerdings nicht mehr viel zu sehen. Viele wurden mit Kiefern oder fremdländischen Douglasien zugepflanzt, andere wurden einplaniert oder als Baustoff abgetragen. Heute ist man bemüht, die Dünenlandschaft wieder behutsam sichtbar zu machen bzw. zu rekonstruieren.

How Lake Steinhude was formed

From a geological perspective, Lake Steinhude is a young body of water. It is about 12,000 years old as it was created after the last Ice Age. Even though the ice layer did not extend to our regions, the soil here was permanently frozen like, for example, today in northern Scandinavia or Russia. As the ice retreated from Central Europe, a previously hidden ice lens in the soil melted, the terrain sagged creating the Lake Steinhude sink. Eventually, winds blew the sand out of the basin so that it accumulated in the form of sand dunes on the Northern shore. There are still more than 60 sand dunes of which the "Weiße Düne" ("White Dune") is by far the largest. However, most of the dunes can no longer be seen today. Pines or exotic Douglas firs were planted on some, while others were levelled or used as building material. Today, efforts are being made to carefully reveal or reconstruct the dunes.

Der Naturpark in seiner Ausdehnung
Expansion of the nature reserve

Heute ist das Steinhuder Meer ohne Frage der Mittelpunkt des gleichnamigen Naturparks, der von Mariensee im Norden bis Wölpinghausen im Süden reicht und ein beliebter Ort für Freizeitaktivitäten ist. Vor allem aber ist der See, an vielen Stellen noch sehr natürlich, trotz der vielen menschlichen Eingriffe, angefangen von kilometerlangen Uferbefestigungen an Nord- und Südufer bis zur aufgeschütteten Badeinsel, wo zuvor ein Schilfmeer wuchs. Seit Jahrtausenden ist er ein wichtiger Lebensraum für eine Vielzahl von Tieren und Pflanzen, eine wichtige Drehscheibe des internationalen Vogelzuges. Tausende von Wat- und Wasservögeln leben ganzjährig oder zumindest zu einem Teil ihres Lebens im Gebiet. Haubentaucher, Tafelenten und Blässhühner zum Beispiel leben hier ganzjährig, zumindest so lange sie trotz Eis und Schnee an ihre Nahrung gelangen. Zusätzlich zu den brütenden Löffel-, Spieß-, Krick-, Knäk-, Pfeif-, und Schnatterenten rasten auf dem Wasser zahlreiche ihrer Artgenossen auf dem Zug zwischen ihren Brutplätzen im Norden und Osten Europas und ihren Winterquartieren, die im Westen oder Süden Europas oder gar in Afrika liegen. Andere Arten wie die hübschen Gänse- und Zwergsäger oder die Blässgänse suchen das Steinhuder Meer auf, um hier den Winter zu verbringen. Zwischen Herbst und Frühling sind besonders viele Vögel auf der Seefläche zu sehen, manchmal bis zu 35.000 gleichzeitig! Dazu kommen allabendlich zahlreiche Möwen, die auf den umliegenden Feldern und Wiesen tagsüber bis zu 50 km entfernt vom Steinhuder Meer Nahrung gesucht haben, wie Wissenschaftler anhand von individuell markierten Vögeln feststellen konnten.

Today, Lake Steinhude is undoubtedly the centre of the Nature Reserve of the same name, which extends from Mariensee in the north to Wölpinghausen in the south and is a popular spot for sports and recreation activities. Most importantly, however, the natural condition of the lake has been preserved at many places, despite numerous human interventions, such as bank reinforcements on the northern and southern shores that extend over several kilometres, or the artificial bathing island, which was built where once there was a lake of reeds.
For millennia, it has been an important habitat for a variety of animals and plants, and a significant resting spot for migrating birds. Thousands of shore- and waterbirds live in this area throughout the year or at least for a part of their lives. Great Crested Grebes, Pochards and Coots, for example, live here all year, at least as long as they can find food in spite of ice and snow. Apart from Shovellers, Northern Pintails, Teals, Garganeys, Wigeons and Gadwalls that breed here, numerous other birds rest on these waters on their long journey between their breeding grounds in Northern and Eastern Europe and their winter quarters in Western or Southern Europe, or as far away as Africa. Other species, such as the lovely Goosanders and Smews or the Great White-fronted Geese spend the winter at Lake Steinhude. Between autumn and spring, an abundance of birds can be spotted on the lake surface, sometimes up to 35,000 simultaneously! Every night, they are joined by a great number of Seagulls that, during the day, were looking for food in the surrounding fields and meadows up to 50 km away from Lake Steinhude, which scientists have been able to track as they marked some of the birds.

Die schneeweißen, grazilen Silberreiher sind seit dem Jahr 2000 regelmäßige Gäste am Steinhuder Meer. Noch vor etwa 100 Jahren waren sie weltweit fast ausgerottet, weil Teile ihres Gefieders als Hutschmuck benutzt wurden
Since 2000, the graceful snow-white Great Egrets have been regular guests at Lake Steinhude. Only about 100 years ago, they were nearly extinct worldwide, as some of their feathers were very popular as hat decoration

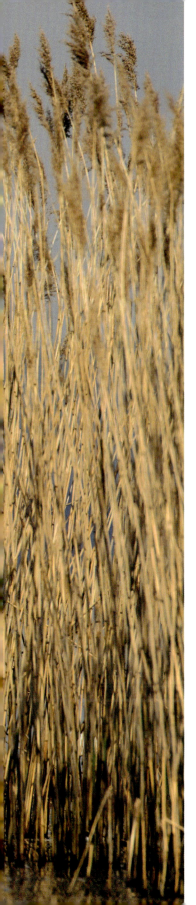

Links: Der Charaktervogel des Steinhuder Meeres ist der Haubentaucher. Im Frühling zeigen die Vögel ein imposantes Balzspiel
Left: The Great Crested Grebe is the characteristic bird of Lake Steinhude. In spring, it is possible to watch the impressive courtship display of the birds

Oben: Die Familenbande der Kraniche hält im Winter. Die beiden Eltern bewachen ihren Jungvogel (links) bis zur Brutsaison im März oder April. Dann schließt sich der Jungvogel anderen Junggesellen an
Top: Crane families stay close throughout winter. Both parents watch their young (left) until the breeding season in March or April. Then the young bird will join up with other bachelors

Seit fast 100 Jahren ist der Europäische Nerz nicht nur in Deutschland ausgestorben. Am Steinhuder Meer gelang es mittlerweile, ihn wieder anzusiedeln
For nearly 100 years, the European Mink has been extinct not only in Germany. Efforts to resettle it at Lake Steinhude have been successful

Seltene Tiere

Nicht nur Vögel leben im und am See. Seit einigen Jahren leben beispielsweise wieder Fischotter am Steinhuder Meer. Sie waren noch in den 1960er und 1970er Jahren als Konkurrenten der Fischerei verfolgt und – zusätzlich unter der erheblichen Gewässerverschmutzung leidend – in den Grenzen der Bundesrepublik fast komplett ausgerottet worden. Nach Unterschutzstellung erholte sich der Restbestand mühsam und im Zuge der Wiederausbreitung erreichten die Otter 2010 das Steinhuder Meer. Sie verrieten sich, als sie durch eine Fotofalle liefen, die von Mitarbeitern der Ökologischen Schutzstation Steinhuder Meer (ÖSSM e.V.) aufgestellt worden war.

Anders der Europäische Nerz: Ihm hatte man schon früher zugesetzt und um 1925 sah man die letzten ihrer Art in Deutschland. Sogar in ganz Europa steht die einst weit verbreitete Tierart vor dem Aussterben. Um sie vor der gänzlichen Ausrottung zu retten, werden europaweit verschiedene Schutzprojekte unternommen.

Rare animals

Not only birds live in and around the lake. In recent years, for example, Otters can once again be spotted at Lake Steinhude. In the 1960s and 1970s still, they were hunted ruthlessly as they were seen as competitors for the fish. In addition, they suffered from the effects of significant water pollution, so that they became extinct within the borders of the Federal Republic of Germany. After they had been declared a protected species, the remaining animals slowly recovered and, thanks to efforts undertaken to expand the population, Otters reached Lake Steinhude in 2010.

They revealed themselves when they were caught on a camera set up by staff of the Lake Steinhude Ecological Protection Station (ÖSSM e.V.). The situation of the European Mink was different: It had been hunted mercilessly many years before, and the last of its kind was seen in Germany around 1925. In fact, this once widespread species is almost extinct in entire Europe. In order to save this animal from complete extinction, diverse conservation projects have been launched throughout Europe.

Das Wiesel, auch Hermelin genannt, ist ein eifriger Mäusejäger und im Naturpark Steinhuder Meer weit verbreitet
The Weasel, also known as Ermine, is an avid mouse hunter and very common in Lake Steinhude Nature Reserve

Seite zuvor: Der Steg. Ein beliebter Platz im Seglerverein Großenheidorn, um der untergehenden Sonne zuzuschauen
Previous page: The landing stage. A popular place at Großenheidorn Sailing Club for watching the sunset

Links: Eine der seltensten Vogelarten in Niedersachsen ist der Karmingimpel. Am Steinhuder Meer brüten einige wenige Paare, meist in Staudenbeständen und feuchten Gebüschen, überraschenderweise aber auch – wenn auch selten – in Gärten.
Die Männchen sind erst im Alter von zwei Jahren rot gefärbt. Bis dahin tragen sie ein schlichtbraunes Federkleid, das dem der Weibchen ähnelt
*Left: One of the rarest bird species in Lower Saxony is the Scarlet Rosefinch. A few pairs breed at Lake Steinhude, usually in shrubs and moist thickets. Surprisingly, though rarely, they can also be spotted in gardens.
The males will develop the red colouring not until the age of two. Until then, their plumage is of plain brown colour, similar to that of the females*

Am Steinhuder Meer wird ebenfalls alles für den Erhalt des Europäischen Nerzes getan. Seit 2010 werden die anmutigen Tiere, die man auf keinen Fall mit den größeren und bei uns unerwünschten „Farmnerzen", also den Amerikanischen Minks, verwechseln darf, von Naturschützern am See wieder ausgewildert. Es bleibt zu hoffen, dass diese Tierart vor dem weltweiten Aussterben bewahrt werden kann.

Ob Vogel, Fischotter, Europäischer Nerz oder viele andere Tiere, sie alle haben eines gemeinsam: Für sie ist das Steinhuder Meer mit seinem Nahrungsreichtum überlebenswichtig. Es ist ihr Zuhause und sie sind darauf angewiesen, dass wir ihnen eine gehörige Portion ihres Lebensraumes zugestehen. Das stellt auch Anforderungen an uns Menschen, die nicht für jeden immer leicht zu verstehen sind. Glücklicherweise haben die meisten Menschen zu teilen gelernt, und die Bereitschaft, auf die Natur Rücksicht zu nehmen ist im Allgemeinen groß.

Vom trüben und klaren Wasser
Das Steinhuder Meer unterliegt einem Wechsel zwischen einem Stadium mit trübem Wasser und einem mit klarem Wasser. Im Trübwasserstadium dominieren in der Regel Blaualgen den Wasserkörper. Sie lassen kein Licht bis auf den Boden vordringen und größere Wasserpflanzen sind selten. So war es rund 70 Jahre lang, bis im Mai 1999 der See aus bislang ungeklärten Gründen innerhalb weniger Tage aufklarte. Plötzlich konnte man selbst in den tiefen Bereichen bis auf den Grund blicken. Zwei Jahre später wuchsen erwartungsgemäß riesige Mengen an Wasserpflanzen auf, ausgerechnet dominiert von der unbeliebten Nuttalls-Wasserpest, einer eingeschleppten nordamerikanischen Wasserpflanze. Panik machte sich breit, doch die Wasserpflanzen verschwanden zwei Jahre später wie von Geisterhand, und im Sommer 2003 war der „Spuk" vorbei. Vermutlich waren es die unzähligen Wasservögel, darunter 700 Höckerschwäne, bis zu 10.000 Pfeifenten und über 20.000 Blässhühner, die das Wachstum bremsten und die Pflanzen verdrängten. 2010 trübte der See wieder ein, und so ist es bis heute geblieben.

Efforts for preserving the European Mink have also been undertaken at Lake Steinhude. Since 2010, conservationists have been releasing the graceful animals into the wild. These should not be confused with the American Minks, which are larger and not indigenous to our region. There are hopes that the species can be saved from worldwide extinction.

Whether bird, Otters, European Minks or many other animals: they all have one thing in common: They rely on the variety of food that Lake Steinhude provides for their survival. It is their home and they depend on us to allow them a reasonable part of it as their habitat. This also places demands on us people, something that not everybody is inclined to understand. Fortunately, most people have learned to share and are generally willing to respect nature.

About murky and clear waters
Lake Steinhude fluctuates between a stadium when the water is murky and a stadium when the water is clear. In the murky water stadium, blue-green algae dominate the body of water. They prevent light from penetrating to the ground and large aquatic plants are rare. This had been the case for about 70 years, until May 1999, when the lake cleared up within a few days for reasons that are yet unknown. Suddenly, it was possible to see through to the ground even in areas where the water is deep. Two years later, as was to be expected, huge amounts of water plants started growing, dominated by the unpopular Nuttall's pondweed, an invasive water plant from North America.
Panic spread, but then the water plants almost magically disappeared two years later, and everything was back to normal in the summer of 2003. Most likely, the countless water birds, among them 700 Mute Swans, up to 10,000 Wigeons and over 20,000 Coots, slowed their growth and displaced the plants. In 2010, the lake turned murky again, and has remained in this stage to this day.

Der Meerbruch – Kulturland und Naturlandschaften westlich des Meeres

Zwischen dem Westufer des Steinhuder Meers und dem hübschen Ort Winzlar erstreckt sich in der Steinhuder-Meer-Niederung eine wunderschöne Landschaft aus feuchten, im Winter überschwemmten Wiesen, Röhrichten, vielen Gewässern und kleinen Wäldchen.

Das Gebiet heißt Meerbruch, bestehend aus den als Naturschutzgebiet geschützten „Meerbruchswiesen" und der Verlandungszone des Sees, die als Naturschutzgebiete „Meerbruch" und „Hagenburger Moor" geschützt wird. Fast das gesamte Gebiet liegt auf weichem, sumpfigen Niedermoorboden.

The Meerbruch – cultivated land and natural landscapes to the west of the lake

Between the western shore of Lake Steinhude and the picturesque village of Winzlar, the Lake Steinhude lowland extends, a beautiful landscape made up of humid meadows that are flooded in winter, reed beds, many bodies of water and small wood stands. The area is called "Meerbruch" and comprises the "Meerbruch meadows", a protected conservation area, and the accretion zone of the lake, protected as conservation areas of "Meerbruch" and "Hagenburger Moor". Almost the entire area extends over soft, marshy lowmoor soil.

Links: Vom Vogelturm am Westufer hat man einen herrlichen Blick am Ufer entlang in Richtung Nordufer
Left: The bird watching tower on the western shore of the lake offers a magnificent view along the shore up to the northern shore

Rechts: Dieser Steg durch den Meerbruch führt zum Vogelturm am Westufer
Right: This landing stage leads through Meerbruch conservation area to the bird watching tower on the western shore

Graugänse gehören am Steinhuder Meer und entlang der Leine zu den auffälligsten Vögeln. Das war nicht immer so. Von 1900 bis 1948 waren sie in ganz Niedersachsen ausgestorben. Nach Ansiedlungen durch Jäger vor allem in den 1960er Jahren breiteten sich die Vögel wieder aus und sind heute erfreulicherweise wieder in fast ganz Niedersachsen verbreitet

Greylag Geese are among the most remarkable birds found on Lake Steinhude and along the Leine River. That has not always been the case. From 1900 to 1948, they had become extinct throughout Lower Saxony. Hunters then settled some Greylag Geese here, especially in the 1960s, and the birds spread again. Today, they can once again be found in almost all of Lower Saxony

Gänsewinter
Bei einem Blick über die weitläufigen Wiesen im Naturschutzgebiet Meerbruchswiesen nahe Winzlar fallen uns im Winter die unzähligen graubraunen Rücken der Gänse auf. Sie fühlen sich in den Meerbruchswiesen sehr wohl.
Das über 1.000 Hektar große Naturschutzgebiet gibt ihnen Nahrung und Schutz. In Ruhe fressen, um Energiereserven anzulegen und damit schließlich heil in die arktischen Brutgebiete zu gelangen, das gelingt ihnen hier besser als in den allermeisten Gebieten Deutschlands.

Adler und Große Brachvögel - mit dem Fernglas der Natur auf der Spur
Aber nicht nur die Blässgänse kennen die westlich an das Steinhuder Meer grenzenden Naturschutzgebiete. Auch naturverbundene Menschen kommen hierher und erleben eine ungeheure Vielfalt an Tieren und Pflanzen und erfreuen sich daran.
Viele tragen Kameras mit riesigen Teleobjektiven und haben hier beste Chancen auf einen tierischen Schnappschuss, andere haben Ferngläser und Fernrohre, mit denen sie auch menschenscheue Vögel auf große Distanzen entdecken können.
Und das geht besonders gut aus den Beobachtungshütten und -türmen, die vom Naturpark, den Naturschutzbehörden und der ÖSSM geplant, gebaut und betreut werden.

Goose winter
Taking just one glance across the vast meadows in the Meerbruch meadows conservation area near Winzlar, one notices the countless grey-brown backs of the geese. They enjoy life in the Meerbruch meadows. The more than 1,000 hectare nature reserve offers them food and shelter. Better than in most areas in Germany, they can feed peacefully here and gain energy reserves for the long flight to their Arctic breeding grounds.

Eagles and European Curlews – with binoculars on nature's trail
But not only the Greater White-fronted Geese know the conservation areas on the western border of Lake Steinhude.
Also nature-loving people come here to experience and enjoy the immense variety of animals and plants.
Many carry cameras with impressive telephoto lenses, optimally equipped to get a snapshot of an animal; others come with binoculars and telescopes to spot shyer birds over long distances. This can best be done from the bird watching huts and towers, designed, built and maintained by the nature conservation authorities and the ÖSSM.

Über 280 Vogelarten, 12 Amphibienarten, außerdem seltene Säugetiere wie Fischotter und Wildkatze wurden hier von Biologen bislang nachgewiesen. Unzählige kleinere Tierarten und seltene Pflanzenarten leben hier. Zumeist sind es solche, die auf nasse und feuchte Lebensräume angewiesen sind oder im Wasser der zahlreichen Kleingewässer leben, wie die Larven der Libellen. Besonders stolz sind Naturschützer auch auf die stabilen Bestände seltener Fischarten, die so seltsame Namen wie Schlammpeitzger oder Steinbeißer tragen. Sie sind im großen Steinhuder Meer fast ausgestorben. In den vielen Tümpeln und in den pflanzenreichen Gräben und Bächen, die seit der Unterschutzstellung des Gebietes nicht mehr alljährlich ausgebaggert werden, finden sie eine zusätzliche Heimat.

Ein Blick in die Vergangenheit
Um die ungeheure Artenvielfalt der Meerbruchswiesen verstehen zu können, müssen wir in die Vergangenheit zurückblicken. Als nach der letzten Eiszeit das Steinhuder Meer entstand, reichte der See bis an den Rand des heutigen Ortes Winzlar heran. Im Laufe Tausender Jahre ist das Steinhuder Meer dann von Westen her, also von der Windschattenseite, an der auch heute noch viel Schlamm ablagert, verlandet. Zunächst wuchsen hier nebeneinander und nacheinander Seggensümpfe, Röhrichte und Erlenbruchwälder; absterbendes Pflanzenmaterial bildete eine organische, nährstoffreiche Bodenauflage – ein Niedermoor. Einige Jahrhunderte zuvor begann die wachsende Bevölkerung zunehmend der Natur Fläche abzuringen, indem sie die Wälder rodete und nach und nach die Landschaft entwässerte.

Biologists have already identified more than 280 bird species, 12 amphibian species, and also rare mammals such as otters and wild cats. Countless smaller animals and rare plant species live here. Most of them need wet and moist habitats or live in the waters of the numerous small bodies of water, such as the larvae of dragonflies. Conservationists are especially proud of stable populations of rare fish species with strange names like "Schlammpeitzger" (Weatherfish) or "Steinbeißer" (Spined loach). In the large section of Lake Steinhude, they are almost extinct. They have found their home in the many pools, ditches and little streams with their abundance of plants, as these are no longer dredged every year since the area was declared a protected nature reserve.

A look into the past
In order to understand the immense biodiversity found in the Meerbruch meadows, we have to look back into the past. When Lake Steinhude was formed after the last Ice Age, the lake extended up to the borders of what is today the village of Winzlar. Over thousands of years, Lake Steinhude dried up from the west, i.e. the lee side of the lake, where to this day a lot of sludge accumulates. Initially, sedge swamps, reed beds and alder forests grew here, simultaneously or successively; dead plant material formed an organic, nutrient-rich soil cover – a low moor. Some centuries earlier, the growing population used more and more space of nature, clearing forests and gradually draining the landscape.

Rechts: Tausende Wintergäste – wie die arktischen Blässgänse aus dem Norden Sibiriens – besiedeln die Landschaften am Steinhuder Meer. Störungsfreie Rückzugsräume wie die Meerbruchswiesen ermöglichen ihnen, Energiereserven für den 6-7.000 km langen Rückflug im Frühling anzufressen
Right: Thousands of winter guests – such as the Arctic Greater White-fronted Geese from the north of Siberia – populate the landscapes around Lake Steinhude. Safe havens like the Meerbruch meadows allow them to gain the energy reserves they need for their 6000-7000 km long return flight in spring

Nächste Seite: Wasserfläche in den Meerbruchswiesen am Südwestufer
Next page: An expanse of water in the Meerbruch meadows on the south-western shore of the lake

Dort wo vorher unberührte Wildnis das Bild der Landschaft bestimmte, entstand eine Kulturlandschaft mit nassen Wiesen, die man aufgrund der anfangs geringen Entwässerungsaktivitäten nur ein- bis zweimal im Jahr mähen konnte. Das als Viehfutter nur mäßig wertvolle Material diente vor allem als Stalleinstreu. Bis in die 1950er Jahre war die Nutzung so extensiv und die Entwässerung so unvollkommen, dass das Heu bei Sommerhochwässern hin und wieder komplett überschwemmt wurde und nicht mehr nutzbar war. Dann begann man die Entwässerung zu perfektionieren. Man legte zahlreiche neue Entwässerungsgräben an, schuf einen breiten Ringgraben, den Südbach, der das Gebiet mittig durchschneidet, begradigte die Bäche und verbesserte die Voraussetzungen für eine intensive landwirtschaftliche Nutzung. Allerdings eine Nutzung, die ein Nebeneinander mit den mittlerweile selten gewordenen Pflanzen und Tieren ursprünglicher Feuchtgebiete und extensiv genutzter Wiesenlandschaften nicht mehr ermöglichte. Eine um die andere Art starb aus und viele weitere wären gefolgt, wenn es nicht möglich gewesen wäre, die Uhr um fünf vor zwölf anzuhalten.

Letzte Rettung für die Wiesenbewohner
Die Rettung für Weißstorch, Großen Brachvogel, Bekassine, Moorfrosch und Co. kam 1989, als das Bundesamt für Naturschutz auf einen Antrag des Naturparkes Steinhuder Meer den Beschluss fasste, mit Beteiligung des Landes Niedersachsen und der damaligen Landkreise Hannover, Nienburg und Schaumburg, den Schutz des Gebietes zu fördern und Flächen im Gebiet anzukaufen und zu entwickeln. Noch war es nicht zu spät, denn viele der typischen Feuchtwiesenbewohner lebten noch in Restbeständen im Gebiet, zum Beispiel die bereits erwähnte Bekassine, der Vogel des Jahres 2013, und der Große Brachvogel. Beides langschnabelige Vogelarten, die mit ihren filigranen

A man-made environment was created where previously pristine wilderness dominated. Initially, only little drainage was undertaken and, as a result, the wet meadows could only be mowed once or twice a year. The cut grass had little value as animal feed and was therefore primarily used as stable bedding. Until the 1950s, due to extensive exploitation and relatively imperfect drainage, the hay was occasionally flooded completely during high water in summer and was then no longer usable. This prompted the residents to try to perfect drainage methods. Numerous new drainage ditches were built to create a wide moat, called the Südbach, which cuts through the centre of the area. In addition, streams were straightened and conditions for farming were improved. Unfortunately, this made the coexistence of rare plants and animals indigenous to the original wetlands and extensively used meadows impossible. One species after the other became extinct, and many more would have followed, had it not been for the intense efforts to stop this development before it would be too late.

***Last rescue for meadow residents**
Rescue for the White Stork, Curlew, Common Snipe, Marsh Frog and others arrived in 1989, when the Federal Agency for Nature Conservation, in response to an application submitted by the Lake Steinhude Nature Reserve and with the help of the State of Lower Saxony and the former districts of Hannover, Nienburg and Schaumburg, decided to protect the area and to buy and develop land in it. It was not too late yet, as a few populations of the typical wetland residents still lived here, for example, the Common Snipe, the Bird of the Year 2013, which we have already mentioned, and the Curlew. They are both long-beaked birds that use their delicate beaks to poke for food in moist soils and shallow waters and can only do so in areas where the soil is moist throughout the year. They are unable to find food on drained meadows.*

Wenn im Westen die Sonne untergeht, schlägt die Stunde der Fischotter, Nachtigallen, Laubfrösche, Wachtelkönige, Eulen und auch der Mücken
When the sun goes down in the west, otters, nightingales, tree frogs, corncrakes, owls and also mosquitoes come out

Schnäbeln in feuchten Böden und in flachen Gewässern nach Nahrung stochern und das auch nur dort können, wo die Böden ganzjährig feucht sind. Auf entwässerten Wiesen gelingt ihnen das nicht.

Zehn Jahre nach Projektbeginn waren 70 Prozent des Grünlandes von den Landkreisen gekauft und so durch Tausch zusammen gelegt, dass man in der Kernzone große zusammenhängende Flächen wieder vernässen konnte.

Der Wasserstand wird heute mit vielen Stauanlagen so geregelt, dass eine landwirtschaftliche Nutzung noch möglich ist. Die Landwirte bekamen die öffentlichen Flächen, die als Grünland extensiv weitergenutzt werden sollten, verpachtet. Der Deal: Sie müssen sich an die naturschutzfachlichen Auflagen halten, wie z. B. an das Verbot von Gülledüngung und den Einsatz von Pflanzenschutzmitteln. Dafür müssen sie aber keinen Pachtzins bezahlen und dürfen die EU-Flächenprämie kassieren.

Viele sinnvolle und bedeutende Naturschutzmaßnahmen folgten dem Ankauf. Wichtige Nahrungsgewässer wurden angelegt, kleine Wege gesperrt und der Rundweg zum Teil verlegt, sodass Rückzugsräume auch für die scheuesten Tiere geschaffen werden konnten. So konnte man die meisten Pflanzen und Tierarten vor dem Aussterben retten.

Zusätzlich schuf man durch den Bau der bereits erwähnten Beobachtungshütten und -türme für die Besucher erstklassige Möglichkeiten, Natur zu erleben. Manche Maßnahmen waren dabei anfangs durchaus unpopulär, vor allem die Verlegung des Rundweges erhitzte die Gemüter. Heute sind die damaligen Gegner ebenfalls überzeugt von dem Konzept, einerseits Natur auf einem hohen Niveau und auf einer fachlichen, wissenschaftlichen Basis zu schützen, andererseits Besucher zu lenken und ihnen scheue Tiere zu zeigen, die sich ohne Lenkung gar nicht hätten ansiedeln können.

Kormorane brüten nicht am Steinhuder Meer, dennoch sind sie hier als Gäste regelmäßig zu sehen, zur Zugzeit auch in großer Zahl. Mit ausgebreiteten Flügeln trocknen sie ihr Gefieder
Cormorants do not breed on Lake Steinhude, yet they can regularly be spotted here as guests, even in large numbers during the migration season. They spread their wings to dry their feathers

Der inzwischen unter Naturschutz stehende Fischotter, einer der besten Schwimmer unter den Landraubtieren, fühlt sich auch am Steinhuder Meer wieder heimisch
The Otter, now a protected species and one of the best swimmers among land predators, once again feels at home at Lake Steinhude

Nächste Seite: Naturbelassene Feuchtwiesen westlich des Steinhuder Meeres
Next page: Undeveloped wetlands west of Lake Steinhude

Ten years after the project was launched, 70 percent of the grassland had been bought from the districts, which were then exchanged for other areas and combined to create a large continuous core zone that could be watered. Many damming structures control the water level so that agricultural use is still possible. The public areas intended for extensive use were leased to farmers. The deal: They had to comply with the nature conservation requirements, such as the ban on manure fertilization and the use of pesticides. In exchange, they did not have to pay rent and were still entitled to collect EU area payments. Many sensible and significant conservation measures followed the purchase of the land. Important food providing waters were created, small paths were closed and parts of the walking trail were moved to create refuge even for the shyest animals. Thanks to these measures, it was possible to save most plant and animal species from extinction.

In addition, bird watching huts and towers were constructed from where visitors could optimally experience nature. In the beginning, some of the measures were quite unpopular, especially the relocation of the walking trail was highly controversial. Today, however, those who initially opposed the idea have been convinced of the concept of protecting nature at a high standard and on a technical, scientific basis, on the one hand, while guiding visitors and showing them shy animals that would otherwise not have settled here, on the other.

Lohn für die Naturschützer: Fischadler, die in unserer Kulturlandschaft nur selten geeignete Nistmöglichkeiten finden, siedelten sich 2006 am Steinhuder Meer auf einer speziellen Nisthilfe an und brüteten das erste Mal seit über 100 Jahren. 2014 zogen bereits vier erfolgreiche Paare (von nur elf in ganz Niedersachsen!) insgesamt elf Jungvögel auf – allesamt auf eigens für die Art konstruierten Nisthilfen

The reward for conservationists: Ospreys that rarely find suitable nesting sites in our cultural landscape, settled at Lake Steinhude in 2006 on a special nesting structure, breeding here for the first time in more than 100 years. In 2014, four successful pairs (of only eleven in entire Lower Saxony!) bred eleven young birds in total – all of them on nesting structures specially erected for these birds

Zu den sich angesiedelten Arten gehören beispielweise Kranich, See- und Fischadler. Sie brüten heute sogar im Meerbruch, was man sich 20 Jahre zuvor nicht vorstellen konnte. Heute ist der Meerbruch sogar das einzige Gebiet im Land, in dem man von einer Stelle in die Nester zweier Adlerarten schauen kann – aus gebührender Entfernung natürlich und mit Hilfe eines Münzfernrohres, sollte man kein eigenes Fernglas dabei haben.

Die Adler vom Steinhuder Meer
Apropos Adler: Die Seeadler brüteten erstmals im Jahr 2000 nach über 100 Jahren am Steinhuder Meer. Das derzeit wohl bekannteste Seeadlerpaar in Niedersachsen schichtete die ersten Äste für das weithin sichtbare Nest im Meerbruch im November 2008 auf und brütete 2009 erfolgreich.

Returned species include Cranes, White-tailed Eagles and Ospreys, for example. Today, these even breed in the Meerbruch conservation area, something that would have been unimaginable only 20 years ago. Today, Meerbruch is the only region in the state where you can look into the nests of two Eagle species from one same place – from a safe distance, of course, and using a coin-operated telescope, in case you did not bring your own binoculars.

The Eagles of Lake Steinhude
Speaking of Eagles: White-tailed Eagles bred at Lake Steinhude for the first time in 2000 after more than 100 years. In 2008, the currently best-known pair of Eagles in Lower Saxony started layering branches for the nest in the Meerbruch, which is visible from afar, and their young hatched successfully in 2009.

Der Seeadler ist mit bis zu 2,4 m Flügelspannweite der größte Greifvogel Deutschlands. Im Jahr 2000 waren die Adler nach vielen Jahrzehnten zurück an Niedersachsens größtem See und zogen erfolgreich den ersten Jungvogel auf

With a wingspan of up to 2.4 m, the White-tailed Eagle is the largest bird of prey in Germany. In 2000, the Eagles had returned to Lower Saxony's largest lake after many decades and successfully bred their first young

Seitdem leben Seeadler hier – mit Blick auf das Steinhuder Meer. Sie sind ein echter Besuchermagnet.

2011 siedelten sich zur Freude der Naturschützer und Besucher auch Fischadler im Meerbruch an, auf einer Nisthilfe, die die Mitarbeiter der Ökologischen Schutzstation Steinhuder Meer (ÖSSM e.V.) zwei Jahre zuvor eigens für die Vögel aufgestellt hatten. Im Jahr 2006 brütete die Vogelart erstmals am Steinhuder Meer, ebenfalls nach über 100-jähriger Abwesenheit. Beide Arten gehören wie auch Fischotter, Kranich, Zwergdommel, Flussseeschwalbe, Wachtelkönig und andere zu den Tierarten, die aufgrund von zahlreichen Schutzmaßnahmen heute wieder im Meerbruch leben können und aus eigener Kraft zurückgekehrt sind. Weniger mobile Tierarten wie beispielsweise der Laubfrosch konnten das nicht schaffen, zu weit sind heute die nächsten Vorkommen entfernt und zu viele Straßen sind unüberquerbare Hindernisse. Für den grünen Baumkletterer kamen alle Naturschutzbemühungen zu spät, er starb in den 1970er Jahren aus, nachdem die letzten Laichgewässer vernichtet worden waren. 2005 startete die ÖSSM ein Wiederansiedlungsprojekt, das sehr erfolgreich verlief. Heute leben im Meerbruch wieder Tausende der in ganz Niedersachsen stark gefährdeten, charismatischen Frösche, neben den vom Naturschutzbund Deutschland (NABU) ebenfalls wieder angesiedelten Europäischen Sumpfschildkröten, unserer einzigen heimischen Schildkrötenart.

Since then, White-tailed Eagles have been living here – enjoying the view of Lake Steinhude. They are real crowd-pullers. In 2011, to the delight of conservationists and visitors, Ospreys also started settling in Meerbruch, using a nesting structure specially built for them by the employees of Lake Steinhude Ecological Protection Station (ÖSSM e.V.) two years earlier. In 2006, this bird species bred at Lake Steinhude for the first time again after more than 100 years of absence. Both species, as well as Otters, Cranes, Little Bitterns, Common Terns, Corncrakes and others, are among those that have returned on their own and can once again live in Meerbruch thanks to numerous conservation efforts. Less mobile species, such as the Tree Frog, on the other hand, were not able to do so as the closest populations were too far away and the large number of roads would have represented obstacles impossible for them to cross. Unfortunately, all conservation efforts came too late for the green tree climbers, and they became extinct in the 1970s after the last of their spawning grounds had been destroyed. In 2005, the ÖSSM launched a very successful reintroduction project. Today, thousands of these charming amphibians, which are endangered in entire Lower Saxony, live once again in Meerbruch, joined by the European Pond Turtle, our only native turtle species, which was also successfully reintroduced by the German Nature and Biodiversity Conservation Union (NABU).

Auch Nutztiere fühlen sich am Steinhuder Meer wohl
Even farm animals seem very happy at Lake Steinhude

Oben: Der Eisvogel gehört zu den besonders bunten und schillernden Arten unter den heimischen Vögeln. Er brütet in Höhlen, die er in Steilwände und in den Wurzeltellern umgefallener Bäume gräbt
Top: The Kingfisher is one of the most colourful and alluring species among indigenous birds. It breeds in caves that it digs in steep walls and in the root plates of fallen trees

Links: Die Bekassine gehört zu den Schnepfenvögeln und wird wegen ihrer meckernden Lautäußerungen auch „Himmelsziege" genannt. Sie war im Naturpark beinahe verschwunden. Naturschutzmaßnahmen, vor allem die Wiedervernässung von Mooren und Wiesen, bewahrten den „Vogel des Jahres 2013" bei uns vor dem Aussterben
Left: Because of its bleating call, the Common Snipe is also called "Himmelsziege" (Sky Goat). It had almost disappeared from the nature reserve. Through conservation measures, especially the rewetting of moors and meadows, it was possible to save the "Bird of the Year 2013" from extinction

Rechts: Der so genannte Seerosenteich liegt östlich des Steinhuder Meeres. Er entstand in einer Abgrabungsstelle. Den dort entnommenen Sand verwendete man zum Bau der Moorstraße
Right: The so-called Water Lily Pond is situated east of Lake Steinhude. It was formed in an excavation pit. The removed sand was used to build the Moorstraße (Moor Road)

Moor

Text: Thomas Brandt

The Moor at Lake Steinhude

Gar nicht gruselig – das Tote Moor
Östlich des Steinhuder Meeres erstreckt sich über eine 30 km² große Fläche – das Tote Moor. Das Moor ist damit etwa so groß wie der See und ebenfalls aus einem eigenen See entstanden. Hier verlief der Jahrtausende während Verlandungsprozess schneller als im Steinhuder Meer. Aus dem See entstand zunächst ein Niedermoor und aus diesem wuchs in mehreren Tausend Jahren, wie Moorprofile erkennen lassen, ein Hochmoor empor, und damit ein ganz anderer, besonderer Lebensraum. Hochmoore werden nur vom Regenwasser gespeist und haben somit einen eigenen Wasserhaushalt. Sie sind durch eine undurchlässige Schicht vom Grundwasser getrennt. Deswegen werden sie auch Regenmoore genannt. Sie sind nährstoffarm, und da der organische Boden vor allem aus unvollständig verwitterten Pflanzenteilen, z.B. den Torfmoosen, besteht, ist er und das Wasser überwiegend sauer. Hochmoore zeichnen sich durch starke tägliche Temperaturschwankungen aus. 20-30 Grad Temperaturunterschied innerhalb eines Tages sind nicht selten.

Not scary at all – the Dead Moor
To the east of Lake Steinhude, the "Tote Moor" (Dead Moor) extends over an area of 30 km². The moor is thus about the same size as the lake and was also formed from a – different – lake. Here, the silting process, which endured over millennia, was completed faster than in Lake Steinhude. Moor profiles indicate that initially a fen was formed from the lake, which then developed into a raised or peat bog over several thousand years, creating a completely different, very special habitat. Raised bogs are fed only by rainwater and thus have their own hydrologic balance. They are separated from the groundwater by an impermeable layer. For this reason, they are also called rainwater bogs. They are low in nutrients, and as the organic soil consists mainly of incompletely decayed plant parts, such as peat moss, the soil and the water are mostly acidic. Raised bogs are characterized by significant daily temperature variations. Temperature differences of between 20-30 degrees in a single day are not uncommon.

Der Mittlere Sonnentau ist eine fleischfressende Pflanze. Die zierliche Azurjungfer hat sich in einem unachtsamen Moment auf die Blätter mit den klebrigen Tropfen gesetzt und wird nicht mehr entkommen
The oblong-leaved sundew is an insectivorous plant. In a careless moment, the tiny Azure Damselfly has sat down on the leaves that excrete a sticky mucilage. It will not be able to escape

Intakte Hochmoore sind offene Landschaften mit nur wenigen Bäumen und Büschen.
Es ist ein extremer Lebensraum, in dem nur wenige Tier- und Pflanzenarten, die sich unter diesen unwirtlichen Bedingungen zu behaupten verstehen, leben können. Aber diese sind Spezialisten, wie zum Beispiel die beiden Sonnentauarten, der Mittlere und der Rundblättrige Sonnentau, die die Nährstoffarmut des Hochmoores bewältigen, indem sie Fliegen und andere kleine Insekten mit Hilfe einer klebrigen Flüssigkeit an ihren Blättern fangen und „verspeisen".
Aber die für diesen Extremlebensraum bestens angepassten Tiere und Pflanzen haben ein Problem. Sie können fast nirgendwo anders leben und ihr Lebensraum wurde in der Vergangenheit stärker zerstört als fast alle anderen in Mitteleuropa. Nur noch rund 1 Prozent der ursprünglichen Moorfläche ist in Niedersachsen, dem hochmoorreichsten Bundesland, unberührt geblieben. Auch das Tote Moor hat gelitten. Seit Jahrhunderten wurde aus dem Hochmoor Torf abgebaut und als Brenntorf oder Dünger verwendet. Ein kleiner Kanal, der heute in Resten noch auf dem Weg zum Beobachtungsturm am Ostufer zu sehen ist, diente dazu, den Torf aus dem Moor nach Steinhude mit Booten abfahren zu können. Es folgten Zeiten des industriellen Torfabbaus, der zunehmend intensiviert wurde. Heute klaffen riesige Wunden im Toten Moor, die links und rechts der Moorstraße zwischen Mardorf und Neustadt zu erkennen sind. Große braune Abbauflächen erstrecken sich hier, sie sind die wirklich toten Flächen im Toten Moor. Heute dient der Torf nicht mehr dem Überleben, sondern wird zu Blumenerde verarbeitet.

Naturschützer haben nur kleine Flächen vor dem Abbau bewahren können. Ihr Ziel ist es, die Hochmoorreste so natürlich wie möglich wieder zu vernässen und die seltene Fauna und Flora zu erhalten. Das wäre dringend erforderlich, will man die Spezialisten der Moore wie

Ein historisches Foto, das von Torfstechern während ihrer verdienten Pause entstand. Heute wird diese Arbeit von Maschinen erledigt
A historic photograph showing peat cutters during their deserved break. Today, their work is done by machines

Rechts: Diese historische Aufnahme eines schwerbeladenen Torfkahnes erklärt das heutige Vorhandensein der zahlreichen Kanäle am Steinhuder Meer
Right: This historic photograph of a heavily laden peat barge explains the presence of numerous channels at Lake Steinhude

Intact raised bogs are open landscapes with only few trees and bushes. It is an extreme habitat with harsh conditions in which only few animal and plant species can live. But these are specialists, like for example the oblong-leaved and the round-leaved sundew. This plant species overcomes the low nutrient content of the bog by "eating" flies and other small insects that it catches with a sticky mucilage excreted from its leaves.

Animals and plants which have optimally adapted to this extreme habitat have one problem: While they are unable to live almost anywhere else, they have seen the destruction of their habitat in the past to an extent found almost nowhere else in Central Europe. Only about 1 percent of the original moor area in Lower Saxony, which is the German state with the largest number of raised bogs, is still intact. Also the Dead Moor has suffered. For centuries, peat had been extracted from the raised bog and used as fuel or as fertilizer. A small channel was used to transport the peat by boat from the bog to Steinhude. Remnants of the channel are still visible along the trail leading to the game watching tower on the eastern shore.

In later periods, peat extraction was increasingly intensified on an industrial level. Today, huge gaping wounds are well visible in the Dead Moor on the left and on the right side of the moor road between Mardorf and Neustadt. Here, vast brown extraction areas extend, and they are the real dead areas of the Dead Moor. Today, people no longer depend on peat for their survival, instead it is processed into potting soil.

Conservationists could only save small areas from excavation. Their goal is to rewet the peat bogs as naturally as possible to preserve the rare fauna and flora. This is urgently required, if we wish to preserve moor specialists, such as the European Adder, Smooth Snake, sundew, cranberry and bog rosemary. Suggestions for different utilisation of exhausted bog areas, on the other hand, are not very productive.

Links: Der zum Denkmal erklärte historische Torfkahn liegt in unmittelbarer Nähe des Vogelturms am Ostenmeer
Left: This historic peat barge has been declared a protected heritage item. It can be viewed near the bird watching tower at the Eastern Lake

Kreuzottern sind bei uns selten geworden. Schuld daran ist der Verlust ihrer Lebensräume durch Abtorfung. Ein kleiner Teil der Kreuzotterpopulation im Toten Moor ist blauschwarz gefärbt, das arttypische Zickzackband auf dem Rücken ist nur zu erahnen
Adders have become rare in our regions due to the loss of their habitats as a result of peat excavation. A small portion of the Adder population in the Dead Moor has a bluish black colour, making the typical zigzag stripe on the back hardly visible

Kreuzotter, Schlingnatter, Sonnentau, Moosbeere und Rosmarinheide erhalten. Wenig zielführend sind Stimmen, die eine Umnutzung abgebauter Hochmoorflächen fordern.

Vielfalt auf dem zweiten Blick
Auf den ersten Blick sieht eine natürliche Hochmoorfläche, wie wir sie nur kleinräumig kennen, sehr strukturarm aus. Das täuscht. Nuancen unterschiedlicher Feuchtigkeit bestimmen die Verteilung vieler Pflanzenarten. Dort, wo es sehr nass ist oder wo gar offenes Wasser steht, leben die rund ein Dutzend verschiedenen Torfmoose – selbstverständlich nicht durcheinander, sondern nach Feuchtigkeitsgrad sortiert. Die sogenannten Roten Torfmoose mögen es am trockensten und überwachsen die, die als Pioniere die nassen Stellen erobern konnten. Auf den Torfmoosschichten wachsen das Schmalblättrige Wollgras mit den baumwollartigen Früchten, die zierlichen Moosbeeren, die übrigens heimische Verwandte der aus Nordamerika stammenden Cranberries sind, das Weiße Schnabelried und an manchen Stellen eine der beiden Sonnentauarten.

Noch etwas trockener mögen es die weißlich und rosa blühende Rosmarin- und Glockenheide. Dort, wo schließlich Besenheide und Rauschebeere wachsen, ist das Hochmoor verhältnismäßig trocken.

Diversity at second glance
At first glance, a natural peat bog area, as we know it on a limited scale, appears to be of poor structure.

This is a misconception. Nuances of different levels of humidity determine the distribution of many plant species. Around a dozen different peat mosses can be found in areas where it is very wet or where there is stagnant water. Not mixed, of course, but sorted by level of humidity. The so-called red peat moss prefers very dry spots, overgrowing those moss species that have spread into the wetter spots. On the peat moss layers, cotton grass with its cotton-like seed heads, delicate cranberries, which are, incidentally, local relatives of the well-known North America cranberries, the white beak-sedge and, in some places, one of the two sundew species grow. Bog-rosemary and cross-leaved heath with their white and pink flowers prefer even drier areas. And in areas where common heather and bog bilberry grow, the raised bog is relatively dry.

An den Stellen, an denen alle der eben erwähnten Pflanzen wachsen, ist die Hochmoorwelt in Ordnung. Meist aber sehen wir Moorbirken und Kiefern. Sie zeigen uns, dass hier zuvor der empfindliche Wasserhaushalt aus dem Lot gebracht wurde. Die typischen Pflanzen der Hochmoore sind verschwunden und damit auch spezialisierte Tiere wie Goldregenpfeifer, Kreuzotter, Hochmoorgelbling oder Hochmoorbläuling. Sie alle finden sich auf der Liste der gefährdeten Tierarten. Glücklicherweise gibt es wieder etwas Hoffnung für den Lebensraum der Hochmoore. Schöne, wieder vernässte Flächen lassen sich heute vom Wunstorfer Damm aus einsehen. Hier kann man wieder einen Hauch der viel beschriebenen Mystik spüren und verstehen – am besten während eines Spaziergangs im frühen Morgennebel.

The growth of all the above-mentioned plants is an indication that the high moor world is still intact. However, what we mostly see are downy birches and pines. They are clear signs that the sensitive water balance was damaged in the past. The typical plants of raised bogs have disappeared, and with them also specialized fauna such as the European Golden Plover, the Adder, or butterflies such as the moorland clouded yellow or the cranberry blue.
All of these are found on the list of endangered species. Fortunately, there is once again a little hope for the habitat of the high moors. Beautiful, rewetted areas can now be seen from the Wunstorf dam. Here, you can experience an air of the much described mystery – and the best way to do this is during a walk in the early morning mist.

Das weiß fruchtende Scheidige Wollgras im Wechsel mit Torfmoos gefüllten Schlenken bedeutet, dass sich hier wieder ein fast natürliches Hochmoor entwickelt
Sheathed cottongrass with its white seed heads alternating with depressions filled with peat moss indicate that an almost natural raised bog has developed here

Wasser ist das Lebenselixier des Hochmoores. Dort, wo Entwässerungsgräben geschlossen werden konnten und wo heute das Wasser steht, werden die unerwünschten Birken durch ein sich entwickelndes Moor abgelöst
Water is the lifeblood of the high moor. Where drainage ditches were closed and stagnating water has formed, the unwanted birch trees have been replaced by a developing bog

Meer Sport

Text: Matthias Beilken

Sports by the lake

Das Meer prägt. Es hat etwas melancholisches. Etwas respekteinflößendes. Es kann einen in voller Bandbreite erwischen. Wie mich, früher ein junger Segler: vormittags Schule, nachmittags Segeln. Ich kenne die meisten Gesichter des Meeres. Stundenlanges, ödes Training, bei dem das Meer kein Festtags-Make-up, sondern lediglich eine eintönige und flaue, graue Maske zur Schau trug. Manchmal hatte sein mooriges Wasser, das nach einer Mischung aus Torf und Schlamm schmeckte, und nicht nach Salz und großer weiter Welt, etwas provinzielles.
Dass das Meer bei diesigem Alltags-Schmuddelwetter einfach nur so dalag, wie eine riesige, einsame und unberührte Wasserfläche, hatte dann etwas melancholisches.

Aber wenn bei Regatten ein peitschender Nordwest einem ins Gesicht biss, wenn die Blinkanlagen am Ufer mit orangen Blitzen vor Sturm warnten, wenn die Wellen groß, grün und böse genug wirkten, als wollten sie einen ersäufen.

The lake forms a person. It has something melancholic. It has something daunting. It can hit you with full force. As it did to me, when I was a young sailor: school in the morning, sailing in the afternoon. I know most of the faces of the lake. Long hours of dreary training, when the lake does not wear its festive make-up, but has put on a monotonous and dull, grey mask instead. Sometimes, its boggy water that tasted like a mixture of peat and mud, instead of salt and the big wide world, seemed a bit provincial.
The fact that the lake just lay there in this dreary, wet weather we had every day, like a huge, lonely and pristine water surface, had something melancholic.

But when, during a regatta, the north-west wind mercilessly hit your face, when the orange lights of the beacons on the shore were flashing storm warning, when the waves seemed large, green and nasty enough as if they wanted to drown you.

Dieter und Andreas Broer vom YSTM holen während einer Regatta in der Flaute raus, was nur geht
Dieter and Andreas Broer of YSTM trying to make the most of a lull during a regatta

Seite zuvor: Großes, ruhiges Meer – einsam zieht eine Jolle ihre Runden
Previous page: The lake, vast and calm – a lonely dinghy sails peacefully away

Oben: Heißes, ruhiges Meer! An manchen Tagen ist kein Wind – aber Sonne
Above: The lake, hot and calm! During some days there is no wind – but sun

Wenn der Himmel nur zerrissene und dahinjagende Wolken zeigte, wenn das Herz bis zum Hals pochte, Durst und Erschöpfung groß, aber nicht zu merken, waren. Wenn hinter der Lee-Ecke des Wilhelmstein der einzige friedvolle Ort auf vielen Quadratkilometern schien, der Flaute und etwas Entspannung bot. Wenn uns an jedem anderen Fleck des Meeres das Wetter um die Ohren flog und uns die grünen Wellen spülten, als wollten sie uns weggurgeln. Dann hatte das Meer auf einmal etwas Herausforderndes, ja Feindseliges.

Wassersport, was ist das eigentlich? Zuerst einmal ist es ein Paar von ungleichen Begriffen. Wasser und Sport: Wasser sediert und beruhigt die Sinne. Als Wettkampf betrieben, putscht Sport aber auf. Klar soweit. Aber was ist „Wassersport in Steinhude"? Was macht das Besondere daran aus?

Viele Menschen begeben sich ausschließlich der Entspannung und der Beruhigung der Sinne wegen in Wassernähe. Aber auch ohne Wettkampf betrieben sie natürlich „Wassersport". Einige Wassersportler betonen eben eindeutig das Teilwort „Wasser" vor dem Teilwort „Sport".

When you saw nothing but torn and chasing clouds in the sky, when your heart was beating vigorously, when thirst and fatigue were severe, but not felt. When the leeward corner of Wilhelmstein fortress seemed to be the only peaceful place where some quiet and rest could be found in many square kilometres. When anywhere else on the lake, the weather blew so violently against our faces and the green waves flushed over us as if they could not wait to carry us away. Then, all of a sudden, the lake had something challenging, even hostile.

Water sports, what is that? First of all, the two terms don't seem to fit together at all. Water and sports: Water calms and soothes the senses. Sports, on the other hand, when done as a competition, charges you up. That's sorted then. But what is "water sports in Steinhude"? What is so special about it?

Many people go near water only when they search for relaxation and calm. But even when there is no competition, they practice "water sports", of course. Some water sports enthusiasts put the emphasis on the "water" part and not on the "sports" part of the word.

Segel-Sonntagsausflug mit der kompletten Familie auf einem P-Boot
A Sunday sailing outing with the entire family on a P-boat

Matthias Kiel im P-Boot mit Vorschoter Andreas Müh an der Luvtonne
Matthias Kiel in the P-boat with foredeck hand Andreas Müh at the windward mark

Links: Start! Wenn jetzt einer der Steuerleute der Jollenkreuzer falsch zuckt, gibt's Kleinholz
Left: Start! If one of the helmsmen on the dinghy cruisers makes just one wrong move, there will be havoc

Was die „Wasserbetoner", die eben auch Sport betreiben, nicht suchen: Zusätzliche Magengeschwüre, wie Leistungsdruck und Wettkampfstress sie fördern können. Aber es gibt sie zuhauf, die „Leistungssportler", die exakt diese Herausforderung suchen. Seit Urzeiten ist das Steinhuder Meer ein Sammelhort für Menschen, die Wochenende für Wochenende das Teilwort „Sport" dem Teilwort „Wasser" vorziehen. Leistungsmenschen sehnen sich natürlich nicht primär nach der Ruhe am Wasser, obwohl auch sie sich dem Zauber des Steinhuder Meers nicht entziehen können. Immerhin gibt es Regattasegler, die jahrein, jahraus immer wieder ans Meer kommen, weil sie es für eins der tauglichsten Jollenreviere Europas halten.

Dazu passt, dass Piraten-Altmeister Frank Schönfeld – der natürlich ewig oft in Steinhude gesegelt ist – auf seiner legendären CD singt: „... er fährt nach Steinhude, und sie putzt ihm die Bude".

The last thing that those who put the emphasis on "water" want to have is more stomach ulcers caused by the pressure to perform and by competition stress. The "competitive athletes", on the other hand, look exactly for this challenge, and you see them everywhere. Since time immemorial, Lake Steinhude has been a place where hoards of people who put the emphasis on "sports" instead of "water" come together one weekend after the next. Those highly ambitious people, of course, are not looking for relaxation by the water – though not even they can escape the magic of Lake Steinhude. After all, there are regatta sailors who keep coming back to the lake year after year because they consider it one of the best spots for dinghies in Europe. Fittingly, Frank Schönfeld, veteran champion in pirate dinghy racing – and who, of course, has sailed on Lake Steinhude many times – sings on his legendary CD: "... er fährt nach Steinhude / und sie putzt ihm die Bude". – ("... he goes to Lake Steinhude and sails, while she cleans the house and wails.")

Das mit dem Begriffspaar „Wasser" und „Sport" wäre geklärt. Was ist denn aber nun „Wassersport auf dem Steinhuder Meer", was macht ihn so speziell? Warum ist Segeln, Kiten, Eissegeln oder Windsurfen seit über einem Jahrhundert als Freizeitvergnügen fester Bestandteil des Lebens am Meer?

So we have sorted out the "water" and "sports" parts. But what is "water sports on Lake Steinhude", what makes it so special? Why has sailing, kiting, ice sailing and windsurfing been a firm part of life at the lake for over a century?

Flautenhalse. Die Kamera in Tiefstellung suggeriert mehr Wind als tatsächlich weht
A jibe manoeuvre in a lull. The low camera position suggests more wind than is actually blowing

Rechts: Wer Böenstriche lesen kann, ist klar im Vorteil! Auf Vorwindkursen richtig zu taktieren ist schwierig, aber entscheidend für eine Regatta
Right: The ability to read the gusts is a clear advantage! Manoeuvring on a downwind leg is difficult, but essential in a regatta

Das Meer ist zeitlos. 100 Jahre mehr oder weniger scheint ihm kaum etwas auszumachen. Boote, die etwa zu Weimarer- oder zu Nachkriegszeiten auf dem Meer herumsegelten, sehen heute noch fast genauso aus, wie damals. Die ganzen alteingesessenen Bootsklassen, die früher schon da waren – wie Jollenkreuzer, H-Jollen, Zugvögel, Korsare oder Hansajollen – segeln noch ihre Regatten und Meisterschaften aus, ergänzt nur durch neue Klassen der jungen Wilden: Europes und 420er, Katamarane, 505er. Egal, Segler aller Altersklassen, alle sind dem Meer offensichtlich ähnlich verfallen wie ich.

The lake is timeless. 100 years more or less hardly seem to make any difference. Boats that sailed on the lake during the Weimar or post-war periods, today look almost exactly as they did then. All the established boat classes that existed in the past – such as dinghy cruisers, H-dinghies, "Zugvögel", Corsairs or Hansa dinghies – are still sailing in regattas and championships, while new classes of the young guns have also been added: Europes and 420s, catamarans, 505s. It doesn't matter – sailors are of all ages, and all have apparently fallen under the spell of the lake, just like me.

Rechts: Dave Seidel auf „Gecko": P-Boot-Vorschoter haben die übelsten Jobs von allen Seglern – und daher einen eindeutigen Spitznamen wie „Schotte" oder „Galeerensklave"!
Right: Dave Seidel on the "Gecko": Foredeck hands on P-boats have the worst jobs of all sailors – hence their nicknames "Scots" or "galley slaves"!

Rechts: P-Boote in der Flaute auf Vorwindkurs
Right: P-boats in a lull going downwind

Ganz rechts: Familiensport Jollenkreuzer – Jörg Dohle und Frau Elena in trauter Zweisamkeit an Bord ihres P-Bootes
Far right: Family sports on a cruiser dinghy – Jörg Dohle and his wife Elena enjoy each other's company aboard their P-boat

Blondes have more fun ... Der Moment an der Luvtonne, kurz bevor der Spinnaker gezogen wird
Blondes have more fun ... The moment at the windward mark, just before the spinnaker is pulled up

Ganz Links: Start! Das Maß „Handbreit" entscheidet! Bei den jungen Seglern geht die Pumpe
Far left: Start! "Six inches" make the difference! The young sailor's hearts are beating fast

Links: Das Feld zieht unter Spinnaker zur Leetonne
Left: The field sails under spinnaker to the leeward mark

Wohl schon oft haben sich Regattasegler über Böenstriche und Winddreher geärgert, die einfach fehl am Platz waren. In solchen Momenten war das Meer gemein zu ihnen. Aber letzen Endes ist das Meer zu niemandem gemein, es ist einfach nur gleichgültig. Wie alle großen Meere. Das macht das Steinhuder Meer so speziell: es benimmt sich wie ein großes.

Probably, regatta sailors have often been annoyed by gusts and wind shifts that occurred just at the wrong place, at the wrong time. In these moments, the lake was simply mean to them. But in the end, the lake is not mean to anybody, it simply doesn't care. Like all large oceans. That makes Lake Steinhude so special: it behaves like the real sea.

Links: Eine 420er Jugendjolle, GER 50906 mit Viola Henkel (WVH) am Ruder und Mathes Schwebe (WVW) im Trapez auf dem Weg zur Luvtonne. Wie alle anderen Fotos auf dieser Doppelseite, waren es Teilnehmer der Deutschen Jugendmeisterschaft 2011 der 420er, ausgerichtet vom Segler-Verein Großenheidorn
Left: A 420-class dinghy, GER 50906 with Viola Henkel (WVH) at the helm and Mathes Schwebe (WVW) on the wire on route to windward mark. This and all the other photographs on this double page show participants at the German Youth Championship in 2011, in the 420 class dinghies, organized by the Großenheidorn Sailing Club

Etabliert: Klaus Antrecht und Sohn Alexander segeln seit Jahren gemeinsam Zugvogel
Established: Klaus Antrecht and his son Alexander have sailed together on their "Keel-Zugvogel" sailing dinghy for years

Ebenfalls etabliert: Zugvogel „Nummer Eins" segelt seit 1961 von Steinhude aus. Darstellung in einem Gemälde von Marinemaler Uwe Lütgen
Also established: "Zugvogel" sailing dinghy "Number one" has sailed from Steinhude since 1961. Here it is shown in a painting by marine painter Uwe Lütgen

Segelnachwuchs der Welt: Auch in der Jugendmeisterschaftsklasse Europe drängelt er sich
Young sailors from different parts of the world: Many have come to participate in the Europe Youth Championship class

Die Größe, die Weite, die Hitze, die Sommerfrische. Die Magie des fast wellenlosen Wassers. Das packt sogar alte Haudegen. Ich erinnere mich, dass einmal „draußen"– außerhalb des Meers – in Region und Kommune erbitterte Wahlkämpfe abgingen. Natürlich lief alles auf einen großen Showdown an einem Wahlsonntag hinaus. Es war ein heißer und flauer Sommertag. Aber anstatt in irgendwelchen Wahlkampf- oder Parteibüros zu sitzen und zu debattieren, fuhr der noch-und-wohl-bald-wieder-Bürgermeister seelenruhig allein mit seiner alten H-Jolle auf's Meer hinaus, als ob er von dort aus den Wahlausgang noch beeinflussen könnte. Voilà, gelebte Meer-Sucht, Seelen-Sedation in Reinkultur.
Das funktioniert: Ich erinnere mich da an ein eigenes Erlebnis. Ich weiß nicht mehr, wer wem was nachgetan hat, der Herr Bürgermeister mir oder umgekehrt. Aber irgendwann als Jüngling kam ich einmal von ausgedehnten Atlantik-Lehr-Segelfahrten zurück. Und um mich nach Monaten angemessen mit meiner Heimat zu versöhnen, habe ich leise und mutterseelenallein in meinem Verein, der Schaumburg-Lippischen Seglervereinigung in Steinhude, einen alten Laser aufgetakelt und habe einsame Runden über das seichte Meer gedreht. Erst danach war ich wieder zu Hause.

Auch wusste ich damals: Erst der Moment, nachdem ich den seichten Ufersaum im Heckwasser des Lasers sehen würde und den Saum, an dem man weder Schwert noch Ruder voll fieren konnte, ohne Schlick aufzuwühlen, ja, erst dieser Moment würde bedeuten, dass ich wieder auf dem Meer bin. Apropos: Die notorische Eigenschaft – Seichtigkeit und Schlickigkeit – hält hartnäckig größere Boote vom Meer fern, weil es ab über einmeterfünfzig Tiefgang heißt „Schwerter zu Pflugscharen". Auch diese Eigenart macht das Meer speziell.

The size, the vastness, the summer feeling. The magic of the almost waveless water. Even old warhorses can't resist it. I remember that once "in the outside world" – beyond the lake – a fierce municipal election campaign was going on. As was to be expected, everything culminated in a major showdown on election day. It was a hot and dull summer day. But instead of sitting and debating in some election campaign or party offices, the current and most likely soon to be re-elected mayor sailed out on the lake on his H-dinghy, dead calm and alone, as if he could influence the election result from there. There you have it: lived lake addiction, pure soul sedation. And it works, as I remember from own experience. I don't know who did it first: the mayor or me. But once, when I was young, I came back from a long instructional sailing trip on the Atlantic. To reconcile myself with my home in due manner after many months spent away, I went to my old club, the Lippische Seglervereinigung in Steinhude, and rigged up an old laser, silently and completely by myself, making lonely rounds on the shallow lake.

Only after that had I truly arrived home.

And I knew exactly: Only once I would see the shallow shoreline in the stern wash of the laser, this shoreline in that you could lower neither centreboard nor rudder without stirring up the mud, yes, only then would I know that I have returned to the lake. By the way: The notorious characteristics – shallowness and muddiness – persistently keep larger boats away from the lake, because draughts of one metre and fifty turn "centreboards into ploughshares". Another characteristic that makes the lake special.

Wind, Riesensegel und keine Welle: So schön kann Windsurfen sein
Wind, giant sails and no waves: windsurfing at its best

Ein Großteil des Steinhuder-Meer-Zaubers, der einen jungen Menschen so nachhaltig prägen kann, entfaltet sich im Winter! Wenn das Eis kommt. Wenn das Meer anfängt zu singen. Weil die riesigen Eisscheiben aneinander reiben und sich geräuschvoll zurechträkeln. Dann krabbeln die Menschen – wie nach einer Erlösung von Agonie nach monatelangem Herbstschmuddelwetter – wieder aus ihren Löchern. Spaziergänger, die einfach nur in klirrender klarer Kälte auf der riesigen gefrorenen Eisfläche spazieren gehen wollen.

Festes oder flüssiges Wasser: Wo ist der Unterschied? Mancherlei „Wassersport" funktioniert ganzjährig, Windsurfen, Eissegeln, Kiten. Es ist schon eine ausgemachte Schande, dass ich weder das Eine, noch das Andere, noch das Dritte gelernt habe. Für jeden der Sportarten ist das Meer nämlich ein Paradies. Als sei es für Gaudi geradezu erfunden worden.

Much of the magic of Lake Steinhude that leaves such a lasting impact on a young person, unfolds in winter! When the ice is here. When the lake starts singing. Because the huge sheets of ice rub against each other while noisily sprawling into place. Then people come crawling out of their holes again – as if delivered from agony after long months of dreadful autumn weather. Promenaders who just want to walk on the vast frozen ice surface in the freezing cold.

Solid or liquid water: What's the difference? Some "water sports" – wind surfing, ice sailing, kiting – can be practised all year round. Sadly, I have to admit that I don't master any of the three, which is a disgrace as the lake is a paradise for each. As if it was invented for having fun.

Oben: Wintertraum – Eishockey vor Großenheidorn
Top: Winter dream – ice hockey in front of Großenheidorn

Spiegeleis: Eine „Eisyacht" der XVer Klasse – entwickelt von Erik von Holst 1932
*Mirroring ice: A XV class "ice yacht" – designed by Erik von Holst in 1932
Watersports*

Ganz Rechts: Dorf-Rowdytum – Surfsegel als Schlittschuhlauf-Windantrieb
Far right: Village hooliganism – surf sails serve as wind propulsion for ice skating

Seite zuvor: Im Kite-Gebiet am Nordufer: Hier geht die Post ab!
Previous page: In the kiting area on the northern shore: flying off!

Wilde Akrobatik: Werksfahrer und Athlet Vito Brabetz mehr in der Luft als im Wasser ...
Wild acrobatics: factory racer and athlete Vito Brabetz, more in the air than in the water ...

Damals im Sommer schien unsere halbe Schülerschaft nachmittags (Schulschwänzer auch schon vormittags) auf der Badeinsel herumzulümmeln. Sehr zu meinem Nachteil – denn coole Surferjungs waren auch damals schon bei den Mädchen angesagt.

Von nur hüftseichtem Wasser umgeben, empfahl sich die künstlich aufgeschüttete Badeinsel als ideales Anfängerrevier. Und da der Wind meist aus dem westlichen Sektor bläst, ergibt sich, wenn er stark genug ist, quer übers Meer eine perfekte Bretterstrecke. Halber Wind hin, halber Wind zurück. Gradlinige Rasestrecke: etwa drei Kilometer, bis wieder Ufer im Weg ist. Dann umdrehen – wenden oder halsen – und wieder drei Kilometer zurück brettern.

Back in the summer, it seemed as if half of the students of our school spent their afternoons (class bunkers already in the mornings) on the island. Much to my disadvantage – because even in those days girls were only interested in the cool surfer dudes.

Surrounded by merely waist-high water, the artificially created bathing island was ideal for beginners. And when the wind that usually blew from the west was strong enough, the lake's surface was simply perfect for sailing. Half wind out, half wind back. A straight racing track: you have about three kilometres before the shore gets in the way again. Then reverse – turn or jibe – and off you go three kilometres back.

...und landet wundersamerweise richtigherum
... and miraculously landing right side up

Steinhuder Meer, was wärest Du ohne Deine Sonnenuntergänge? Diesmal im Yachtclub Steinhuder Meer in Großenheidorn
Lake Steinhude, what would you be without your sunsets? Here at Lake Steinhude Yacht Club in Großenheidorn

Ich kann nicht umhin, zu vermuten, dass meine Freunde mit ihren Boards höllischen Spaß hatten – und mit den Mädchen auch. Und wir dagegen machten uns mit unserem schweren Regattapiraten Sorgen um unsere sportliche Karrieren! Ob die Erfolge den Spaß kompensieren konnten, den die andern hatten?

Wer die Zone knietiefen Wassers hinter sich gelassen und besagte drei Kilometer lange Bretterstrecke in Angriff genommen hatte, kam ohne Zweifel am Norduferstrand im Bereich der Weißen Düne an. Dort, wo sich aus der damaligen Nordufer-Subkultur eine bis heute sehr aktive, offizielle Surfer-Hochkultur etablierte. Denn heute agieren Wind- und Kitesurfer in einem eigens eingetonnten Areal.
Wenn man sich heute diesem Gebiet unter Segeln nähert, reicht es nicht mehr, wie früher, auf das Wasser vor dem Boot zu achten. Die Luftzone über der Wasserfläche ist genauso wichtig. Denn es könnte sein, das da etwas angeflogen kommt. Entweder fliegt ein Kitesurfer gerade durch die Luft oder er schickt die Halteschnüre seines Drachens den Ereignissen, die sein Brett gleich einlösen wird, voraus. Gerade in dieser neuartigen Sportart wird so manches geboten.

Subkultursport braucht keine alteingessenen Vereine. Segler brauchen sie. Vereine, deren Mitglieder und Vorstände sich – immer wieder und in variablen Lautstärken – über den Zustand des Meeres, Verschlammung und knietiefen Ufersaum beklagen. Vor allem der Seichtigkeit wegen aber lachen sich Windsurfer – und neuerdings auch Kiter – ins Fäustchen, weil genau diese für sie ideal ist. Und eine weitere Gruppe Wassersportler freut sich über ideale Bedingungen: Katamaransegler. Die Freizeit-Doppelrumpffreaks haben das Meer seit Jahrzehnten ins Herz geschlossen. Ihre Boote haben oft keine Schwerter. Und wie bei den Windsurfern entspricht die riesige freie Wasserfläche des Meeres ihrem enormen Geschwindigkeitspotenzial. Auch für Katsegler scheint das Meer wie gemacht.

I guess my friends also had one hell of a time with their boards – and also with the girls. We, on the other hand, with our heavy regatta pirate dinghies, were worrying about our sporting careers! Could our later successes compensate for the fun the others had?

Once you left the zone of knee-deep water behind and tackled said three-kilometre racing route, you would undoubtedly arrive on the northern shore of the beach in the area of the White Dune. Here, the former northern shore subculture has evolved into an official high surfer culture, which is very active even today. Nowadays, wind and kite surfers can practice in a designated buoyed area.
When you approach this area on your sailing boat today, you have to watch not only the water in front of the boat but also the air zone above the water surface. You never know when something comes flying. Either a kite surfer flies straight through the air, or he throws the wires of his kite ahead for his board to follow. This new sport has much to offer.

Subculture sports don't need old-established clubs. Sailors, on the other hand, do. Clubs whose members and committees keep complaining about the state of the lake, the siltation and the knee-deep shoreline – again and again and at different volume levels. But it is exactly the lake's shallowness that makes it so attractive and ideal for wind surfers – and more recently also for kiters. Another group of water sports enthusiasts that thrive in these conditions are catamaran sailors. For decades, the lake has taken the hearts of these leisure-time double-hull freaks. Their boats often have no centreboards. And like the windsurfers, the vast open water fits their enormous speed potential. As if the lake was made for catamaran sailors.

...und ohne Deine Stege!
... and without your landing stages!

Auch ich erlebte meinen Mehrrumpf-Initationsritus am Meer.

Für uns Dorfjungs waren Kats anfangs jedoch suspekt. 1987 veranstaltete der Yachtclub Steinhuder Meer (YSTM) in Großenheidorn eine Europameisterschaft der Dart-18-Katamarane mit über 80 Schiffen. Die brauchten massig Platz. Großer Sport oder Vereinsmeierei? Beides.

I also experienced my multi-hull rite at the lake.

To us village boys, catamarans were initially suspicious. In 1987, the Yacht Club Steinhude (YSTM) in Großenheidorn organized a European Championship of Dart 18 catamarans with over 80 boats. They need lots of space. Great sports or clubby culture? Both.

Mininachwuchs: Kids segeln Opti. Erst einzeln zu zweit ...
Our minis: Kids sailing on an Opti. First two in one ...

... und dann zu zweit einzeln
... then two in two

Rechts: Auf dem schönen Gelände des SVG in Großenheidorn
Right: On the beautiful grounds of the Sailing Club Großenheidorn

Ist kein Wind, wird gepaddelt
If there's no wind, we have to paddle

„Après-sail-party" allein
"Après-sail-party" alone

Katamarane der Marke Topcat, K1 (18 Fuss) und K3
(16 Fuss) auf einer Amwind-Kreuz auf dem Weg zur
Wendemarke im Gegenlicht
*Topcat K1 (18 feet) and K3 (16 feet) catamarans close
hauled en route to windward mark into the sun*

Michael Winkelmann mit seinem Vorschoter Matthias Holl
auf ihrem Topcat K1 während einer Trimmfahrt
*Michael Winkelmann with his foredeck hand Matthias Holl on
their Topcat K1 catamaran on a trim cruise*

Jeden Sommer stellt jeweils einer der Vereine Wochenende für Wochenende offiziell massig Platz und Raum zur Verfügung, für die vielen zugereisten Regattasegler, die hier ihre Zelte aufschlagen. Denn manchmal hat Wassersport auch was mit Camping zu tun: Regattasegler sind auf der Jagd nach Ranglistenpunkten fast jedes Wochenende woanders unterwegs und auf Campingeffizienz angewiesen, denn Camping ist für Segler kein Selbstzweck. Die Regattasaisons am Steinhuder Meer funktionieren jahrein, jahraus ähnlich, einige Events sind sehr prestigeträchtig: Der Sieg beim „Nesselblatt", der Finn-Dinghys, beispielsweise garantiert ähnliche Anerkennung wie ein Sieg bei der Kieler Woche. Es gibt eine sehr aktive Wettfahrtvereinigung am Steinhuder Meer, die die Regatten und Meisterschaften quasi zentral verwaltet.

Da passiert manchmal Ulkiges. 1987 beispielsweise hatte der Hannoversche Yachtclub die Deutsche Meisterschaft im Piraten in Steinhude auszurichten. An einem der Grillabende hatte ein armer Kerl eine Wette verloren und sollte deswegen in die knietiefe, schlammige Brühe geworfen werden. Ich sprudelte darauf schadenfrohe Worte, die ich wahrscheinlich lieber ungesagt gelassen hätte: „Hihi, fier weg, den Heini!" Die offiziellen Heini-Schubser formierten sich bereits, das Werk sollte prompt vollbracht werden. Aber aus der dunklen Grabbelmasse hinter mir schoss plötzlich eine Hand (ich weiß immer noch nicht, wem sie gehörte) und schob mich flugs über die Kante des Stegs unterm Kran. Platsch, ab ins Schlammwasser.

Ein Jahr später, im Zusammenhang mit der Pflege meiner sportlichen Karriere, verabredete ich mich 1988 einmal mit einem jungen Spätaussiedler-Polen namens Karol Jablonski, der von seiner Sportschule in Sopot bei Gdynia eine Menge Erfahrung mitbrachte. Es ging um den Umstieg in eine neue Bootsklasse.

Every weekend in summer, one of the clubs provided a huge area where all the participating regatta sailors from other regions could pitch their tents. Because sometimes water sports also has something to do with camping: On the hunt for ranking points, regatta racers travel to a different place almost every weekend and depending on camping efficiency, because for sailors, camping is not end in itself. The regatta season at Lake Steinhude works the same year in, year out, and some events are even quite prestigious: A victory in the Finn dinghy category – the "nettle leaves" – comes with similar recognition as a victory at the Kiel Week. Lake Steinhude boasts a very active racing association that manages the regattas and championships centrally, so to say.

And sometimes funny things happen. In 1987, for example, the Hannover Yacht Club hosted the German championship in pirate dinghy sailing in Steinhude. At one of the barbecues in the evening, a poor fellow had lost a bet and was to be thrown into the knee-deep, muddy broth. That prompted me to blurt out mischievously: "Hee hee, Heini, overboard you go!", which I should probably rather left unsaid. The official Heini pushers were already lining up, the act was to be completed promptly. But, all of a sudden, a hand shot up from the dark mass behind me (to this day I have no idea whose hand it was) and pushed me flying over the edge of the landing stage under the crane. Splash, into the muddy water.

A year later, in 1988, me keeping up with my sporting career, I had an appointment with a young late repatriate from Poland whose name was Karol Jablonski. He had quite a lot of experience from his sports school in Sopot near Gdynia. We discussed the change to a new boat class.

Nicht ganz am Wind: Alter Gaffeljollenkreuzer
Not quite on the wind: An old gaff dinghy cruiser

Karol kannte ich von meinem Nachbarzimmer her, denn dort standen die Hantelbank und die Bauchmuskel-Trainiermaschine. Und der junge Pole kam regelmäßig mit seinem Rennrad (mit dem er vorher eine Runde um das Meer gedreht hatte) in unsere Straße angerast und ließ die Gewichte krachen, während ich in meinem Zimmer nebenan meine Hausaufgaben nicht machte. Ergo: Der dereinstige Segelstar und America's-Cup-Skipper aus Steinhude wusste schon immer, was er wollte, war stets eine Spur ambitionierter als wir und auch etwas aggressiver.

So waren damals auch die besagten Testrunden auf dem Meer bis heute wertvolle und exklusive Lektionen.

Mittlerweile ist Karol neunfacher Weltmeister im Eissegeln. Und die Eissegelgemeinde am Steinhuder Meer – die traditionell sehr stark war – unterscheidet noch heute zwischen einer „Zeit vor Karol" und einer „Zeit nach Karol".

Damals schärfte sich Karol in Steinhude fleißig die Krallen an fast allem, was segelte, vor allem an Jollenkreuzern. Er arbeitete bei Segelmachern und bei der Werft Bopp und Dietrich, wo ich später meinen Minirenner für die Einhandregatta Minitransat überholte. Ein Boot, nicht länger als ein P-Boot, sechseinhalb Meter. Es war eine schöne Zeit damals, in den Dörfern mit Wassersportzentrumsanschluss. Das Meer hat mich geprägt wie kein anderer Ort, den ich je Heimat zu nennen versuchte. Obwohl ich natürlich längst woanders wohne und arbeite und mittlerweile zehn Mal den Atlantik überquert habe, fühle ich mich im Herzen doch noch als kleiner Jollensegler aus dem Dorf. Als kleiner Junge aus Steinhude, der vormittags nach Wunstorf zum Höltygymnasium radelt und nachmittags manchmal einsame Runden über ein großes graues Meer furcht. Oft, wenn ich heute von irgendwo „nach Hause" (wo auch immer das ist) zurückkomme, ist mir noch immer danach, erst einmal eine einsame Runde über das Meer zu drehen.

Die Vollholz H-Jolle Baujahr 1959 (Gründungsjahr des SVG!) des Herausgebers und Mitautors dieses Buches Heinrich K.-M. Hecht im Ostenmeer
The solid-wood H-dinghy, built in 1959 (founding year of the SVG!), of the publisher and co-author of this book, Heinrich K.-M. Hecht, in the Eastern Lake

I knew Karol because he had the room next to mine, complete with weight bench and abdominal muscle trainer. And the young Pole regularly came on his racing bike (after completing a lap around the lake) into our street and pushed some iron, while I was doing my homework next door. Ergo: The later sailing star and America's Cup skipper from Steinhude always knew what he wanted, was always a tad more ambitious than we were, and also a little more aggressive. I treasure mentioned training laps on the lake as valuable and exclusive lessons.

Meanwhile, Karol is nine-time world champion in ice sailing. And, to this day, the ice sailing community at Lake Steinhude – traditionally very strong – makes a distinction between a "time before Karol" and a "time after Karol". When I met him then, Karol was tirelessly sharpening his claws in Steinhude on almost anything that sailed, especially on dinghy cruisers. He worked with sailmakers and at the shipyard Bopp and Dietrich, who later overhauled my Minitransat mini-racer for solo regattas. A boat, not longer than a P-boat, six and a half meters. We had a great time back then, in the villages with en-suite water sports center. The lake has formed me more than any other place I have ever tried to call home. And even though I have long since moved away and work elsewhere, and have crossed the Atlantic ten times, deep in my heart I still see myself as the little dinghy sailor from the village. As the young boy who pedalled on his bike to the Höltygymnasium in Wunstorf in the morning and sometimes ploughed lonely furrows on a vast grey lake. Often today, when I come back "home" from somewhere (wherever that is), I still have the urge to go for a solitary cruise on the lake.

Oben: Fototermin für die Zeitschrift Yacht: Vor Großenheidorn sammeln sich historische Weserjollen ...
Above: Photo session for the magazine "Yacht": historical Weser dinghies gather in front of Großenheidorn ...

Rechts: Sechs Tage lang hat man so ein Motiv im Kopf und dann klappt es auch noch – gemeinsam zur Sonne!
Right: For six days, you carry such a motif in your head and then it actually comes out right – together towards the sun!

Orte am Meer

Text: Emke Hillrichs

Großenheidorn

Towns and villages by the lake

„Zweiteiler am Meer"
Die Ortschaft Großenheidorn ist ein altes, früher zum Fürstentum Schaumburg-Lippe gehörendes Bauerndorf, das sich in reizvoller Wiesenlandschaft nahe des Steinhuder Meeres befindet.
Großenheidorn liegt östlich von Steinhude, welche nahtlos ineinander übergehen. Der wassernahe Ortsteil Großenheidorns, unmittelbar am Steinhuder Meer gelegen, nennt sich Großenheidorn Strand und kann viele attraktive Wohn- und Wochenendhäuser vorweisen.

A "two-in-one town" by the lake
The small town of Großenheidorn is an old farming village that used to be part of the Principality of Schaumburg-Lippe. It is situated in a charming meadow landscape near Lake Steinhude.
Großenheidorn is situated east of Steinhude, the two towns merging seamlessly. The district Großenheidorn Strand (Großheidorn Beach) is located directly at the lakeshore; here, many attractive residential and holiday homes have been built.

Eines der ältesten, noch existierenden Häuser in Großenheidorn. Zu Beginn des 17. Jahrhunderts erbaut und liebevoll von seinen heutigen Eigentümern saniert
One of the oldest still existing houses in Großenheidorn. Built in the early 17th century and lovingly restored by its current owners

Der Segler-Verein Großenheidorn (SVG) und der Yachtclub Steinhuder Meer (YSTM) unterhalten im Ortsteil Großenheidorn Strand ihre Vereinshäuser und Liegeplatzanlagen. Beide Vereine sind weit über die Grenzen hinaus durch ihre Aktivitäten im Jugendbereich und die durchgeführten Regattaveranstaltungen während der Saison bekannt. Viele wichtige Events haben sie schon veranstaltet, darunter Europameisterschaften, zahlreiche Deutsche Meisterschaften, Jugend- und Jüngstenmeisterschaften, die im Auftrag des Deutschen Segler-Verbandes durchgeführt wurden. Welt-, Europa- und Deutsche Meister zählen zu ihren Mitgliedern.
Großenheidorn wurde wahrscheinlich um 1220 gegründet und erstmals 1247 in einer Urkunde von Graf Ludolf von Roden erwähnt, da er dem Bischof von Minden, die beiden Dörfer Großenheidorn und Klein Heidorn zuerkannte.

The Großenheidorn Sailing Club (SVG) and Lake Steinhude Yachting Club (YSTM) have their clubhouses and mooring facilities in the Großenheidorn Strand district. Both clubs are known beyond regional borders for their activities for the youth and for the regattas they organize during the season. On behalf of the German Sailing Association, they have organized many important events, including European Championships, numerous German championships, and also championships for youth and children. World, European and German champions are among their members.
Großenheidorn was probably founded around 1220 and first mentioned in 1247 in a deed issued by Count Ludolf of Roden by that he assigned the two villages Großenheidorn and Klein Heidorn to the Bishop of Minden.

Blick in den Garten und die dahinter liegenden Wiesen des Hauses von Seite 146
A view of the garden of the house pictured on page 146 and the meadows behind it

Die St. Thomas Kirche in Großenheidorn, die im 17. Jahrhundert erbaut wurde, war ursprünglich eine katholische Kirche. Daher der Name, der der Kirche erst in den 90er Jahren von der evangelischen Gemeinde wiedergegeben wurde
St. Thomas Church in Großenheidorn, which was built in the 17th century, was originally a Catholic church. Hence the name, which the Protestant parish only gave back to the church in the 1990s

Der Name des Dorfs geht wahrscheinlich auf das Wort Heithorn zurück, das zu jener Zeit einen Wald mit großen Vorkommen an Weiß- und Schwarzdorn bezeichnete. Das Dorf ging später in den Besitz des Grafen von Holstein-Schaumburg über. Nach dem Aussterben des Adelsgeschlechts, kam es 1640 zur Teilung der Grafschaft Schaumburg.

Großenheidorn wurde zusammen mit Steinhude, Hagenburg, Wölpinghausen, Wiedenbrügge und Schmalenbruch-Windhorn, als sogenannte Seeprovinz dem nordöstlichen Teil zugeschlagen und fortan von den Grafen der Familie Lippe-Detmold regiert. Nach der Abdankung des letzten regierenden Fürsten von Schaumburg-Lippe zum Ende des Ersten Weltkriegs, verblieb Großenheidorn im Freistaat Schaumburg-Lippe. Nach dem Zweiten Weltkrieg gehörte es bis zur Gebietsreform zum Kreis Stadthagen.

The name of the village probably originates from the word "Heithorn" which, at the time, described a forest with a large number of white and blackthorns. The village later became part of the property of the Count of Holstein-Schaumburg. After the last members of the aristocratic family had died, the Principality of Schaumburg was divided in 1640.

Großenheidorn together with Steinhude, Hagenburg, Wölpinghausen, Wiedenbrügge and Schmalenbruch-Windhorn constituted the so-called lake province in the north-east and was henceforth ruled by the Counts of the Lippe-Detmold family. Following the abdication of the last reigning Prince of Schaumburg-Lippe at the end of World War I, Großenheidorn remained part of the Free State of Schaumburg-Lippe. After the Second World War, it belonged to the district of Stadthagen until the local government reform.

Das zu Beginn des 20 Jahrhunderts errichtete Strandhotel in Großenheidorn Strand ist heute das Clubgebäude des Yachtclubs Steinhuder Meer und strahlt auch nach über 100 Jahren noch eine gewisse Würde aus

Built in the early 20th century, the beach hotel in Großenheidorn Strand is now the clubhouse of Lake Steinhude Yachting Club. Even after more than 100 years, it has a certain grandeur

Der Ortsteil Großenheidorn Strand ist von einigen solcher Kanäle durchzogen, die dem Ort eine außergewöhnliche Atmosphäre verleihen
Großenheidorn Strand district is crossed by a few channels like this one, which give the place a unique atmosphere

Von 1898 bis 1970 hatte Großenheidorn auch einen Bahnanschluss an die Steinhuder Meer-Bahn, mit zwei Haltestellen am Dorfkrug Brauner Hirsch (Ortsausgang) und der Gastwirtschaft Küker in der Ortsmitte.
Der Ort liegt in nächster Nähe zum Naturschutzgebiet Wunstorfer Moor (Wulveskuhlen und Ostufer Steinhuder Meer). Auf den umliegenden Wiesen und an den Ufern sind viele zum Teil bedrohte Vogelarten zu entdecken. Die Landzunge von Großenheidorn Strand wird im Sommer viel zum Baden oder als Startpunkt für Surfer und Kanuten genutzt. Eine quirlige Ortschaft, von der Segelfaszination ebenso ausgeht, wie auch dörfliches Leben mit all seinen Facetten.

From 1898 to 1970, Großenheidorn had been connected to the Lake Steinhude Railway, which used to stop at the village pub "Brauner Hirsch" (at the town exit) and at the restaurant Küker in the town centre.
The town is situated in direct vicinity of the Wunstorfer Moor Nature Reserve, which includes the "Wulveskuhlen" and the eastern shore of Lake Steinhude. Many bird species, some of them endangered, can be spotted on the surrounding meadows and along the shores. In summer, many people use the tongue of land of Großenheidorn Strand for swimming or as a starting point for surfing and kayaking. It is a lively town where sailing fascination and also village life in all its facets can be experienced.

Wunstorf

Text: Klaus Fesche

Was die erste urkundliche Erwähnung betrifft, gibt es so viele Städte nicht in Niedersachsen, die mit Wunstorf mithalten können: Schon 871 stellt König Ludwig der Deutsche, das „Stift bei Wuonheresdorpe" unter seinen Schutz. Das Stift – kein Kloster! – war einige Jahre zuvor von Bischof Dietrich von Minden gegründet worden, bei der also schon existierenden Siedlung Wunstorf.
Die Lage zwischen zwei Auearmen sorgte für Schutz und Wasserversorgung; das Stift wurde hochwassersicher auf dem östlich gelegenen „Stiftshügel" errichtet. Seither hat Wunstorf eine wechselvolle, von Höhen und Tiefen geprägte Entwicklung erfahren.

As far as first written mention is concerned, you won't find many towns in Lower Saxony that can keep up with Wunstorf: As early as 871, King Louis "the German" placed the "collegiate church near Wuonheresdorpe" under his protection. The collegiate church, which was not a convent, had been founded a few years earlier by Bishop Dietrich of Minden, in the settlement of Wunstorf, which hence already existed. Its location between two arms of the wetlands ensured protection and water supply; the collegiate church was flood-proof as it had been erected on the "collegiate church hill" in the east. Since then, Wunstorf's history has been quite eventful, marked by many ups and downs.

Frühmorgens an der Westaue ist die Stimmung beizeiten märchenhaft
Early in the morning, the atmosphere in the western wetlands sometimes looks as if taken out of a fairy-tale book

Die romanische Stiftskirche des 871 erstmals erwähnten Stifts Wunstorf liegt idyllisch in der Nähe der Aue, vor deren Hochwassern sie durch ihren Standpunkt auf dem Stiftshügel geschützt war

The Romanesque Wunstorf collegiate church, first mentioned in 871, is idyllically situated near the wetlands. Its location on the hill protected it from floods

Der Aufstieg im Mittelalter ist auch der Rivalität der beiden Stadtherren zu verdanken: Die Herrschaft über Wunstorf teilten sich die Bischöfe von Minden und die Grafen von Roden (später Grafen von Wunstorf) in einem konfliktträchtigen Verhältnis. Die Kontrahenten suchten die Einwohnerschaft auf ihre Seite zu ziehen, indem sie ihr Privilegien einräumten. Bischof Kuno verlieh Wunstorf 1261 das Mindener Stadtrecht, Graf Johann von Roden bewilligte der Stadt 1287 einen Jahrmarkt. Einen Höhepunkt erreichten die Zwistigkeiten zwischen Bischof und Graf in den Jahren 1314 bis 1317, bei dem Ersterer die Oberhand behielt; Rat und Bürgerschaft der Stadt erklärten ihre Treue dem Bischof. Dieser zwang den Grafen, seine Burg in Wunstorf abzubrechen, gestand ihm aber zu, eine neue in Blumenau zu errichten. Der Bischof behielt seine Burg in Bokeloh.

Mitte des 15. Jahrhunderts traten die Herzöge von Braunschweig und Lüneburg die Nachfolge der Grafen in der Herrschaft über die Stadt an – bis zur Reformation gemeinsam mit den Mindener Bischöfen.

To some extent, the town owed its rise in the Middle Ages to the rivalry between the two rulers of the town: The sovereignty over Wunstorf was shared between the Bishops of Minden and the Counts of Roden (later Counts of Wunstorf), and their relationship was marked by many conflicts. Both opponents tried to get the population on their side by granting it certain privileges. In 1261, Bishop Kuno granted Wunstorf the Minden town privilege, while Count Johann of Roden permitted the town to hold a fair in 1287. The disputes between the Bishop and the Count culminated in the years between 1314 and 1317, in which the former prevailed; the town council and the citizens declared their loyalty to the Bishop. He forced the Count to abandon his castle in Wunstorf, but allowed him to build a new one in Blumenau. The Bishop kept his castle in Bokeloh.

In the mid-15th century, the Dukes of Brunswick and Lüneburg succeeded the counts and became the sovereigns of the town – shared with the Bishops of Minden until the Reformation.

Reiterin Christine Tofahrn mit ihrem Pferd „Prime Time" (genannt „Ernie"...) vor dem Rittergut Düendorf. Das Gut stammt aus dem Jahre 1527 und wurde von einem Herrn von Mandelsloh errichtet, der den Boden für 1000 rheinische Gulden vom Grafen zu Wunstorf erwarb. Der damalige Name des Grund und Bodens war „Wüste Dugenthorp". Der heutige Eigentümer Gerd Tofahrn ist der Stiefsohn des letzten Herrn von Mandelsloh

Equestrian Christine Tofahrn with her horse "Primetime" (called "Ernie" ...) in front of the Düendorf Manor. The manor dates back to 1527 and had been built by a certain Lord of Mandelsloh, who had purchased the ground for 1,000 Rhenish guilders from the Count of Wunstorf. In those days, the land was called "Wüste Dugenthorp" (Dugenthorp desert). The current owner Gerd Tofahrn is the stepson of the last Lord of Mandelsloh

Gegenüber dem Mittelalter war die Frühe Neuzeit eine Epoche der Krisen. 1519 wurde die Stadt während der Hildesheimer Stiftsfehde niedergebrannt. 1570 wurde die Stadt durch Ortgies Dove zum großen Teil erneut in Flammen gelegt. Der Kopf des Brandstifters wurde daraufhin in einem eisernen Korb an der Südwestecke des Marktkirchenturms aufgehängt. Dort hängt noch heute eine Nachbildung des Korbs. Der Dreißigjährige Krieg schließlich brachte Wunstorf an den Rand der Auslöschung: Am 21. August 1625 wehrten sich die Wunstorfer gegen Reiter des kaiserlichen Feldherrn Tilly, die ihnen das Vieh wegnehmen wollten. Zur Strafe ließ Tilly die Stadt brandschatzen, 152 Wohnhäuser – neun von zehn! – wurden zerstört. Die Gesamthöhe der Wunstorfer Schäden wurde auf 55.680 Taler geschätzt (was dem Gegenwert von fast 7000 Kühen entsprach).

Einquartierungen und weitere Plünderungen zogen die Stadt noch jahrzehntelang in Mitleidenschaft, und Wunstorf verarmte für lange Zeit. Dies mag der Eindruck des späteren Schweizer Schriftstellers Jeremias Gotthelf illustrieren, der 1821 als Göttinger Student auf einer Reise in die Stadt kam. Er notierte: „Nach einer durch die schlechten Straßen mühevollen Meile gelangten wir endlich nach Wunstorf, ein Nest, das auf den Namen eines Städtchens Anspruch macht." Erst der Eisenbahnbau 1847 und später die Industrialisierung brachten für Wunstorf wieder einen Aufschwung. Ende des 19. Jahrhunderts wurden eine Zementfabrik, ein Margarine-Werk, aus dem sich später eine große Iglo-Niederlassung entwickelte, und anderes mehr gegründet.

Unlike the Middle Ages, the early modern period turned out to be a time of crises. In 1519, the town was burnt down during the Hildesheim Diocesan Feud. And once again in 1570, part of the town was burnt in a fire started by Ortgies Dove. The arsonist's head was hung up in an iron cage at the south-western corner of the market church tower. A replica of the cage is exhibited there today. The Thirty Years' War finally brought Wunstorf to the brink of annihilation: On 21 August 1625, Wunstorf residents resisted horsemen sent by imperial commander Tilly, who wanted to confiscate their cattle. As punishment, Tilly ordered that the town was to be pillaged, and residential houses – nine out of ten! – were destroyed. The total amount of damage suffered by the Wunstorf population was estimated at 55,680 Wunstorf thalers (which was equivalent to the value of nearly 7,000 cows). For many decades after this, the town continued to suffer as a result of quartering and other plundering, and Wunstorf was extremely poor for a long period. Jeremias Gotthelf, who was to become a well-known Swiss author later, visited the town in 1821, when he was a student in Göttingen. He wrote: "After an arduous journey on the bad roads, we finally arrived at Wunstorf, a hole of a place, claiming to be a town." It was only after the construction of the railway in 1847 and later industrialisation that Wunstorf saw another boom. In the late 19th century, a cement factory, a margarine plant, which was later turned into a major branch of Iglo frozen food company, and other businesses were established.

Der Airbus A400M vor dem Ausbildungszentrum des Fliegerhorstes Wunstorf. In dieser Halle werden zukünftig Techniker vom Technischen Ausbildungszentrum der Luftwaffe ausgebildet

The Airbus A400M in front of the training centre of Wunstorf airbase. In this hall, technicians will be trained by the Technical Training Centre of the German Air Force, prospectively

Der A400M ist das neue Transportflugzeug der Luftwaffe. Er wird die Transall C-160 ersetzen. Auf dem Fliegerhorst Wunstorf werden in den nächsten Jahren insgesamt 40 dieser Flugzeuge stationiert. Dafür sind und werden umfangreiche Anpassungen der Infrastruktur vorgenommen

The A400M is the new transport aircraft of the Air Force. It will replace the Transall C-160. In the next few years, 40 of these aircraft are to be stationed at Wunstorf airbase. For this, extensive modifications to the infrastructure have been planned and implemented

Idensen (Wunstorf)

Links: Für ihre Wand- und Deckenmalereien ist die Idenser Sigwardskirche weithin berühmt
Left: The Sigward Church in Idensen is widely famous for its wall and ceiling paintings

Rechts: Bischof Sigward von Minden ließ die Kirche um 1130 als Grabeskirche erbauen; sie ist ein bedeutendes Denkmal romanischer Baukunst
Right: Bishop Sigward of Minden had the church built as a tomb church in 1130; it is an important monument of Romanesque architecture

Auch bedeutsame öffentliche Einrichtungen entstanden: 1875 ein Lehrerseminar (heute Hölty-Gymnasium), 1880 eine Landarmen- und Korrigenden-Anstalt (heute Psychiatrie des Regions-Klinikums) und 1904 die Scharnhorst-Schule. Diese Aufwärtsentwicklung wurde durch den Ersten Weltkrieg gestoppt, dem Inflation und Weltwirtschaftskrise folgten. Während des Nationalsozialismus wurde der Fliegerhorst errichtet und die jüdische Gemeinde der Stadt völlig ausgelöscht.

Nach dem Zweiten Weltkrieg wuchs die Stadt durch Flüchtlinge und Vertriebene bis 1950 von 6000 auf 11000 Einwohner. Stadterweiterungen wurden notwendig – vor allem in Gestalt der Oststadt und der Barne; letztere konzipierte der bekannte Stadtplaner Hans Bernhard Reichow. Mit der Gebietsreform 1974 wurde Wunstorf auf einen Schlag eine Mittelstadt mit rund 40 000 Einwohnern, die sich dem

Other important public institutions were also established: In 1875, a teacher training college (which today is the Hölty-Gymnasium), in 1880, the Correction and Reformatory Institute (today the psychiatric ward of the regional hospital), and in 1904, the Scharnhorst School. This upswing was halted by World War I, followed by the inflation and the Great Depression. During the period of National Socialism, the airbase was built and the Jewish community of the town was completely erased.

After the Second World War, as a result of the influx of refugees and displaced people, the town's population increased from 6,000 to 11,000 in 1950. Town expansions became necessary, which resulted in the building of the Oststadt (East Town) and the Barne. The latter was designed by famous town planner Hans Bernhard Reichow. With the local government reform in 1974, Wunstorf became a medium-sized town with approx. 40,000 inhabitants.

Mesmerode/Wunstorf

Eigentlich nur die Reste des Kaliabbaus, aber für uns Segler am Steinhuder Meer ist es der Kalimandscharo und für Autofahrer und Piloten eine Landmarke
These are actually nothing more than the remains of potash mining. Sailors refer to it as the "Kalimandscharo" (a play on the German word "Kali", which means potash), while it serves as a landmark for motorists and pilots

wirtschaftlichen Wandel anpasst und ihre verkehrsgünstige Lage auszunutzen weiß. Gleichzeitig ist die Kernstadt von einem Kordon reizvoller Dörfer umgeben, allen voran Steinhude mit dem Steinhuder Meer, dessen Wasserfläche vollständig zu Wunstorf gehört. Wer das Meer besucht, besucht Wunstorf – das auch eine schmucke Altstadt mit interessanten Gebäuden zu bieten hat, wie der Stiftskirche und der Abtei, dem Ratskeller, dem Röbbigsturm und der Wasserzucht.

It has adapted to the economic changes and has used its favourable location to its benefit. The core town is surrounded by a cordon of charming villages, most notably Steinhude with Lake Steinhude. The entire water surface of the lake falls under the municipality of Wunstorf. Those who visit the lake will also visit Wunstorf – which boasts a quaint old town with interesting buildings, such as the collegiate church and the abbey, the Ratskeller (town hall cellar), the Röbbig tower, and the historic town centre street "Wasserzucht".

Steinhude

Text: Jürgen Engelmann

Mein Steinhude
Steinhude am Steinhuder Meer, die „Perle" der Region Hannover, früher des Schaumburger Landes, liegt in reizvoller Umgebung am Nordrande des „bergigen Landes", den nördlichen Ausläufern der Mittelgebirge mit Deister, Weserbergland und den Rehburger Bergen. Am Südrand der norddeutschen Tiefebene bettet sich Steinhude ein zwischen den Hügeln nördlich und südlich des Meeres, die als Hinterlassenschaften der Eiszeiten das Landschaftsbild prägen.

Das Leben in Steinhude war und ist geprägt durch die besondere Lage am Meer mit Niedermoor im Westen, Hochmoor im Osten und überwiegend sandigen Hügeln, den Endmoränen der Eiszeit, im Süden. Der See, der wie andere ähnliche Gewässer in Norddeutschland „Meer" (Mare) genannt wurde, gab Möglichkeiten zum Fischen.

My Steinhude
Steinhude on Lake Steinhude, the "pearl" of the Hannover Region, which was once the Principality of Schaumburg, is located in beautiful surroundings on the northern edge of the "mountainous country", the northern foothills of the low mountain range with Deister, Weser Uplands and the Rehburg Mountains. On the southern edge of the North German Plain, Steinhude is embedded between the hills to the north and the lake to the south, where remnants from the Ice Age determine the landscape.

Life in Steinhude is and has always been determined by its special situation on the lake with the fen to the west, the high moor to the east and predominantly sandy hills, the end moraines of the Ice Age, to the south. The lake that, like other similar waters in northern Germany, was called "Meer" (Mare, which actually translates as "sea"), offered opportunities for fishing.

„Auswanderer" – so nennen wir hier die Boote, die zum Schutz gegen Wind und Wetter an der Mole liegen, und sonst ihre Gäste zum Wilhelmstein und Nordufer bringen. Früher fuhren die Schiffe zum Nordufer ins hannoversche Ausland, daher der Name Auswanderer
The typical open dinghies are moored at the pier to protect them against wind and weather. Normally, they transport tourists to Wilhelmstein fortress and to the northern shore. In the past, the northern shore used to be part of the Hannover outland, and thus a foreign state. Hence the name "Auswanderer", which means "emigrants"

Das Land um Steinhude herum, die Moorwiesen und der für Ackerbau nur teilweise geeignete Boden mit vielen kleinen und großen Findlingen im Süden ließ zumindest eine karge Landwirtschaft zu, mit der Möglichkeit aus dem Moor im Osten Torf für den Hausgebrauch zu stechen. Steinhude hat seinen Namen von den Steinen und dem Platz am Wasser – Hude. Steine und die geringen Ackerflächen machten es notwendig, sich auf verschiedene Weise den Lebensunterhalt zu sichern. Zusätzlich zur Landwirtschaft und zur Fischerei entwickelte sich die Weberei. Zunächst als Handweberei, die mit besonderer Fertigkeit und Kunst betrieben wurde. Das „Hemd ohne Naht" und Decken mit Bildmotiven sind im Fischer- und Webermuseum zu bewundern. Fische und Webereierzeugnisse wurden meist von den Frauen mit Kiepen auf langen Fußwegen in die Städte der Umgebung zum Verkauf gebracht. Mit der Mechanisierung und dem Bau der Steinhuder Meer-Bahn entwickelte sich industrielle Weberei, die mit anderen Industriebetrieben (Lederfabrik, Metallwaren, Birkenstock Schuhe) neben vielen Handwerksbetrieben Arbeitsmöglichkeiten bot. Im 20. Jahrhundert wurde Steinhude auch mit den Einkaufsmöglichkeiten zum Zentrum in der Meerregion. Besucher lockte das Meer, der Wilhelmstein und die reizvolle Umgebung schon länger, aber mit dem Bau der Steinhuder Meer-Bahn gab es einen Aufschwung und der „Tourismus" wurde zum wichtigen Erwerbszweig. Ab den 60er Jahren mussten Industriebetriebe schließen, das Handwerk verlor an Bedeutung, sodass Steinhuderinnen und Steinhuder heute im wesentlichen Arbeit in den Städten der Umgebung finden oder vor Ort als Selbständige oder Beschäftigte im Handel und Dienstleistungsbereich für Einwohner und Besucher tätig sind.

Abenddämmerung über der zugefrorenen Gracht vor dem „Alten Winkel" mit der schneebedeckten Promenade dahinter
Dusk over the frozen canal in front of the "Alten Winkel" with the snow-covered promenade

The land around Steinhude, the moorland meadows and the soil, which is only partly suitable for agriculture, with many small and large boulders to the south, at least permitted some meagre agriculture. The moor to the east provided peat that people could use as fuel. The name Steinhude refers to the many stones found in the area and its location near the water, which was called "Hude". Due to the stones and the limited areas of arable land, people had to devise different ways to make a living. Weaving developed as an important craft aside from agriculture and fishing. Initially, people perfected the skill and art of hand weaving. The "seamless shirt" and blankets with elaborate patterns can be viewed in the Fisher and Weaver Museum. Fish and weaving products were sold in the surrounding towns. Normally, women had to carry them in panniers and walk long distances on foot. Mechanization and the construction of the Lake Steinhude Railway resulted in the development of industrial weaving. People could now find work in this and other industries (leather factory, metal goods, Birkenstock shoes). In the 20th century then, Steinhude with its vast shopping possibilities gradually became the centre of the lake region. For some time already, visitors had been attracted by the lake, Wilhelmstein fortress and the beautiful surroundings, but with the construction of the Lake Steinhude Railway came a boom and "tourism" became an important source of income. From the 1960s, industrial businesses were forced to close and the importance of crafts declined, so that today the majority of the Steinhude population works in the surrounding towns, or is self-employed or employed in the trade and services sector serving residents and visitors.

Park am Meer auf dem Ratskellerplatz, wo die Steinhuder seit 1477 einen „freien Ratskeller" haben, und seit 500 Jahren das Braurecht
Park at the lake on the town hall cellar square. Since 1477, Steinhude residents have enjoyed a "free town hall cellar". For 500 years, they have the right to brew beer

Elektroboote und Tretboote stehen zur Fahrt auf dem Steinhuder Meer bereit, unter dem typisch norddeutschen Wolkenhimmel
Electric boats and pedal boats can be used for trips on Lake Steinhude. Above, the typical clouds in the Northern German sky

Die besondere Landschaft zieht viele Besucher, Tagesgäste und Urlauber an, die sich sportlich betätigen oder einfach nur an der Natur erfreuen wollen. Mit größeren Parkplätzen, Promenaden am Meer, der Badeinsel und einem attraktiven Kurpark und Hafenbereich, jeweils mit attraktiven Spielplätzen, ist der Ort auf viele Besucher eingestellt. Auch die Einwohner genießen all die Vorzüge.

Besucher, die nicht aktiv auf dem Meer sind und sich fahren lassen wollen, werden übers Meer zum Wilhelmstein oder zum Nordufer mit den „Auswanderer"-Booten undden Motorbooten der Steinhuder Personenschifffahrt gebracht. Wassersport und die „Landaktivitäten" wie Wandern, Radfahren, Tennis und Golf sind das, was auf und ums Meer herum angesagt ist. Die Badeinsel bietet neben dem Platz zum Sonnen und sportlichen Aktivitäten auch Musikevents zum Sonnenuntergang. Naturerlebnis pur ist es, die Landschaft mit ihrer außergewöhnlichen Vegetation zu genießen und die reiche Tierwelt zu beobachten.

Kultur gibt es in und um Steinhude reichlich.

Die Steinhuder Museen mit Fischer-, Weber- und Spielzeugmuseum zeigen, wie in Steinhude gelebt, gearbeitet und gespielt wurde. In der Kaltmangel wird vorgeführt, wie das fertige Leinen unter tonnenschweren Gewichten geglättet und glänzend wurde. In der Windmühle Paula wird an alten Geräten das Korn aufbereitet und gemahlen, ein mühlentechnisches Museum der besonderen Art. Viele Insekten gibt's im Schmetterlingsmuseum zu bestaunen und in einem speziellen Klimaraum fliegen die Schmetterlinge zu Hunderten um die Besucher herum. Im Ortskern und auf dem Scheunenplatz sind wunderschöne Fachwerkhäuser anzusehen, die mit Sprüchen über den Torbögen auf ihre Entstehung hinweisen. In der Skulpturenmeile am Meer, in Ausstellungen in der Kunstscheune und in den Glashäusern auf dem Wilhelmstein wird Kunst auf besondere Weise geboten.

Musik- und Theaterveranstaltungen auch auf der Seebühne runden das Angebot ab. Nicht zu vergessen die „Esskultur". Mit feiner regionaler Küche und auch mediterranen Angeboten locken Restaurants und Bistros. Die Spezialität „Steinhuder Rauchaal" kann man auch in den Räuchereien direkt aus dem Ofen genießen.

An der Promenade sitzen, aufs Meer sehen und Fischbrötchen oder Eis essen gehört zu den Lieblingsbeschäftigungen der Steinhudefans, dazu gibt es den schönsten Sonnenuntergang der Welt.

The special landscape attracts many visitors, day excursionists and holidaymakers, who wish to do sports or simply enjoy nature. The town has made arrangements to accommodate the great number of visitors, with extended parking areas, promenades by the lake, the bathing island, beautiful spa gardens and a picturesque harbour with attractive playgrounds. But, naturally, all the benefits are also there for the residents to enjoy. Visitors who do not sail themselves are transported across the lake to Wilhelmstein fortress or the northern shore, either in the typical open dinghies, called "Auswanderer", or in the motorboats of Steinhude passenger transport. Water sports and also "land activities" such as hiking, cycling, tennis and golf are very popular at and around the lake. On the bathing island, people can sunbathe, engage in sporting activities, and enjoy music events at sunset. The countryside offers wonderful opportunities to experience pristine nature, an extraordinary vegetation and abundant wildlife. Steinhude also boasts a rich cultural offer. Museums in Steinhude, such as the Fisher, Weaver and Toy Museum, illustrate how people once lived, worked and played in Steinhude. In demonstrations on the cold mangle, visitors can watch how the finished linen used to be smoothed under extremely heavy weights until it shone. The Windmill Paula is a technical museum of a special kind, where the grain is prepared and ground on old machines.

Many insects can be admired in the Butterfly Museum, which includes a special climate-controlled room where butterflies fly around the visitors in their hundreds.

The town centre and the barn square boast many beautiful half-timbered houses. Inscriptions over the doors tell the visitor when the houses were built. Art is presented in a special way along the sculpture mile at the lake, in exhibitions at the Art Barn and in the glasshouses on Wilhelmstein fortress. Music and theatre performances on a floating stage make the offer perfect. And let us not forget the "food culture". Restaurants and bistros offer fine regional and Mediterranean cuisine. The speciality "Steinhude smoked eel" can also be enjoyed straight from the oven at the smokehouses.

Sitting on the promenade, watching the lake, eating fish rolls or ice cream are the favourite pastimes of Steinhude fans. And on top, they can enjoy the most beautiful sunsets in the world.

Hagenburg

Text: Klaus Fesche

Zwar gab Steinhude dem See seinen Namen, doch war lange Zeit Hagenburg der Hauptort am Steinhuder Meer. Wohl zur Sicherung der zahlreichen, von den Grafen von Roden gegründeten Hagensiedlungen des 13. Jahrhunderts errichtet, wurde die Hagenburg erstmals 1378 erwähnt. In den folgenden Jahrhunderten wechselte sie als Pfandobjekt mehrfach den Besitzer, diente also als Gegenleistung und Sicherheit, wenn ihre Eigentümer sich Geld geliehen hatten. Mit der Burg verbunden war der Sitz des schaumburgischen Amtes Hagenburg am Süd- und Westufer des Steinhuder Meeres. Zu den Dörfern dieses Amtes gehörte auch Altenhagen – seit 1970 mit Hagenburg vereint –, das, wie der Name nahelegt, noch deutlich älter als der Burg- und Amtssitz ist. Es dürfte um 1220 entstanden sein und wurde 1247 erstmals genannt, in derselben Urkunde, die auch Großenheidorn, Klein Heidorn, Nordsehl, Lüdersfeld, Lauenhagen und Wiedenbrügge erstmals erwähnt. Amtssitz blieb Hagenburg bis 1885, als es diese Funktion an Stadthagen verlor.

Bemerkenswert ist Hagenburg zudem als Flecken und als Poststation auf der wichtigen Poststraße Hannover-Osnabrück; auf der Durchreise haben hier Monarchen wie Peter der Große, Georg I. von Großbritannien, Gustav von Schweden und die Preußenkönige Friedrich Wilhelm und Friedrich II. halt gemacht.

Even though the lake got its name from Steinhude, Hagenburg had been the major town at the shore of Lake Steinhude for a long time. Hagenburg castle, first mentioned in 1378, was probably built to protect the numerous Hagen settlements, founded by the Counts of Rodenhagen in the 13th century. In subsequent centuries, it changed hands several times as its owners used it as collateral for borrowing money. The castle also served as the headquarters of the Schaumburg district administration of Hagenburg on the southern and western shores of Lake Steinhude. The villages under the jurisdiction of this administration included Altenhagen, which was merged with Hagenburg in 1970. As the name suggests, it is significantly older than the castle and the headquarters. It was probably built around 1220 and was first mentioned in 1247, in the same document in which also the names of Großenheidorn, Klein Heidorn, Nordsehl, Lüdersfeld, Lauenhagen and Wiedenbrügge can first be found. Hagenburg remained the headquarters of the administration until 1885, when it lost this function to Stadthagen.

Hagenburg also held an important position as market town and as coaching inn on the main postal road between Hannover and Osnabrück. Several monarchs stopped here on their journey, among them Peter the Great, George I of Great Britain, Gustav of Sweden and the Prussian Kings Friedrich Wilhelm and Friedrich II.

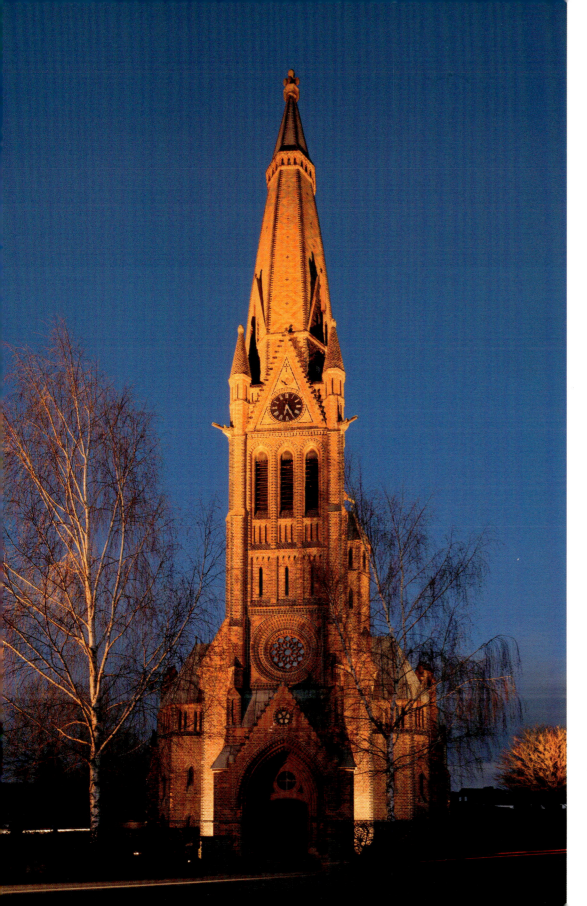

Ein Kleinod neugotischer Baukunst ist die von Christoph Wilhelm Hase erbaute Hagenburger Kirche im Ortsteil Altenhagen
The Hagenburg church in Altenhagen district, built by Christoph Wilhelm Hase, is a gem of Neo-Gothic architecture

Unter Friedrich Christian von Schaumburg-Lippe wurde die Burganlage erweitert und zu einem Schloss umgebaut, gut 100 Jahre später unter Fürstin Juliane noch einmal im klassizistischen Stil umgewandelt. Doch dazwischen hat sie unter Graf Wilhelm eine neue Bedeutung bekommen: Im Rahmen seiner Steinhuder-Meer-Planungen spielte Hagenburg eine wichtige Rolle als Brückenkopf und Verbindungsort zum Wilhelmstein, der auch von hier aus errichtet wurde; im Schloss residierte der Kommandant des Wilhelmsteins. Das benachbarte „Wilhelmsteiner Feld" mit seinen Gärten und Plantagen diente als befestigte Versorgungsbasis für die Inselfestung. Jahrzehntelang starteten Besucher des Wilhelmsteins ihre Überfahrt zur Insel am Hagenburger Schloss, wo sie vorher die Erlaubnis dafür einzuholen hatten.

Erst durch die Steinhude begünstigende Steinhuder Meer-Bahn verlagerte sich das Gewicht des Fremdenverkehrs zugunsten des Fischer- und Weberorts.

Heute gehört Hagenburg-Altenhagen mit rund 4.500 Einwohnern zur Samtgemeinde Sachsenhagen. Neben dem Schloss Hagenburg (heute ein privates Kunst- und Auktionshaus) mit seinem Park, durch den eine schöne Rhododendron-Allee führt, hat der Ort noch weitere Sehenswürdigkeiten aufzuweisen: Etwa den 1561 erbauten Ratskeller, die 1869-71 von Conrad Wilhelm Hase in neugotischem Stil erbaute Kirche St. Nicolai, das Bergbaumuseum in Altenhagen, einen lehrreichen Moor- und einen Findlingsgarten.

Stolz sind die Hagenburger zudem auf ihr seit 1848 gefeiertes Schützenfest, das auch in der gesamten Umgebung sehr beliebt ist – 2 500 Besucher zum abendlichen Tanz sind nichts Ungewöhnliches.

Under Friedrich Christian of Schaumburg-Lippe, the castle complex was enlarged and rebuilt into a palace. About 100 years later, Princess Juliane had it refurbished in the Neo-Classical style. In the period between, though, it had gained new significance under Count Wilhelm: In his plans for Lake Steinhude, Hagenburg played an important role as a bridgehead and connection to Wilhelmstein fortress, which was also built from here; the commander of Wilhelmstein fortress resided in the castle. The neighbouring "Wilhelmstein Field" with its gardens and plantations served as a fortified supply base for the island fortress. For decades, visitors crossed the lake to get to the island from Hagenburg Castle, and also had to obtain a permission there. Only after the Lake Steinhude Railway had been built, did tourism gradually move to the fishermen and weaver town.

Today, Hagenburg-Altenhagen with around 4,500 inhabitants belongs to the joint municipality of Sachsenhagen. Next to Hagenburg Castle (today a private art and auction house) with its park comprising a beautiful rhododendron-lined avenue, other attractions of the town include: the town hall cellar, which was built around 1561; St. Nicolai Church, built by Conrad Wilhelm Hase in the Neo-Gothic style between 1869-71; the Mining Museum in Altenhagen as well as an educational moor and a boulder garden. Hagenburg's inhabitants are especially proud of their "Schützenfest" (marksmen's festival), which has been organized since 1848 and is very popular in the entire area. Often, up to 2,500 visitors come to the evening dance.

Links: Dieser wunderschöne Rhododendron-Gang führt direkt zum Hagenburger Schloß

Left: This beautiful rhododendron passageway leads directly to Hagenburg Castle

Rehburg-Loccum

Text: Klaus Fesche

Die Klosterkirche St. Maria und Georg wurde um die Mitte des 13. Jahrhunderts errichtet
St. Mary and George Minster was built in the mid-13th century

Der um 1300 entstandene Kreuzgang
The cloister dates back to 1300

Ebenfalls aus dem 13. Jahrhundert stammt das große, prächtige Kreuz, welches über dem Altar hängt. Der Chor der Klosterkirche ist wie bei Zisterzienserkirchen üblich als „Kastenchor" mit geradem Abschluss ausgebildet

The magnificent cross above the altar is also from the 13th century. The choir of the minster is designed in rectangular shape, as is typical of Cistercian churches

Rehburg-Loccum ist mit rund 10 000 Einwohnern ein sehr kleines Städtchen – aber dafür reich an Geschichte, Kulturstätten und Sehenswürdigkeiten, die ihm überregionale Bekanntheit verschaffen. Außer dem alten Rehburg – entstanden im Hochmittelalter als Burg und Amtssitz und 1648 mit Stadtrechten ausgestattet – gehören Bad Rehburg, Winzlar, Münchehagen und Kloster Loccum dazu.

Das ursprüngliche Zisterzienserkloster Loccum wurde 1163 als Tochtergründung der Thüringer Abtei Volkenroda errichtet und gestiftet von den Grafen von Hallermund. Es gilt heute als das besterhaltende Zisterzienserkloster nördlich des Mains. Seit 1585 unter welfischer Hoheit, wurde es infolge dessen evangelisch und ist heute eine der wichtigsten Institutionen der hannoverschen Landeskirche; traditionell ist der Landesbischof auch Abt des Klosters Loccum, dessen Aufgabe auch ist, ein Predigerseminar zu unterhalten. Die Evangelische Akademie Loccum, dem Kloster gegenüber gelegen und ebenfalls eine Einrichtung der Landeskirche, ist bekannt für ihre Tagungen zu einem breiten Spektrum gesellschaftlicher Themen.

With a population of just 10,000, Rehburg-Loccum is a very small town – yet it is rich in history, cultural sites and monuments, which have earned its fame beyond regional borders. These include the old Rehburg – which was originally built as a castle in the High Medieval Period and was granted town rights in 1648 – and also Bad Rehburg, Winzlar, Münchehagen and Loccum Monastery.

The original Cistercian monastery Loccum was built in 1163 as daughter house of Vokenroda Abbey in Thüringen; it had been founded by the Count of Hallermund. Today, it is considered the best preserved Cistercian monastery north of the River Main. In 1585, it fell under the sovereignty of the Guelphs and became Protestant. Today, it is one of the most important institutions of the Church of Hannover. Traditionally, the regional bishop is also the abbot of Loccum Monastery, and his responsibilities include the organization of a theological seminary. The Loccum Protestant Academy, located opposite the monastery and also an institution of the regional church, is well known for its conferences on a wide spectrum of social topics.

Bad Rehburg

Text: Klaus Fesche

Eine ganz andere Welt präsentiert sich in Bad Rehburg, das seit der Entdeckung heilender Wasser 1690 zunächst Angehörige des hannoverschen Adels anzog, die Linderung ihrer Leiden suchten. Ab Mitte des 18. Jahrhunderts wurde es zum Bad des hannoverschen Hofs ausgebaut und insbesondere in der Zeit der Romantik erlebte es seine Blüte. Badehaus, Brunnenhaus, Wandelhalle und mehr wurden errichtet, die hannoverschen Hofgärtner gestalteten Garten- und Parkanlagen und lenkten die Aussichten zum Steinhuder Meer. In den Kuranlagen begegneten sich Adel und wohlhabendes Bürgertum so ungezwungen wie sonst nirgendwo. Der spätere hannoversche Archivrat Johann Georg Kestner (bekannt als Ehemann der Lotte aus Goethes „Werther") erlebte hier als junger Mann die „wahre Brunnenfreiheit". Inzwischen restauriert, gilt Bad Rehburg neben Hofgeismar als das einzige noch erhaltene Badeensemble der Romantik in Deutschland, dessen Kurleben ein kleines Bademuseum anschaulich darstellt.

Die Existenz des Bades, die Naturschönheiten in Gestalt der Rehburger Berge, das nahe Steinhuder Meer, die Scharnhorstschule in Wunstorf und nicht zuletzt Geschäfte im Kalibergbau dürften auch den Apotheker Ernst Georg Jünger bewogen haben, 1907 nach Rehburg-Stadt zu ziehen. Seine Söhne Ernst und Friedrich Georg wurden bekannte Schriftsteller, vor allem Ernst, der mit seinem Roman „In Stahlgewittern" über den Ersten Weltkrieg berühmt wurde. Wer aber über die Steinhuder Meer Region während der Kaiserzeit lesen möchte, greife zu Friedrich Georgs Jugenderinnerungen „Grüne Zweige".

Die Friederikenkapelle wurde 1842 vom hannoverschen König Ernst August zum Andenken an seine verstorbene Gemahlin gestiftet
Friederike Chapel was founded in 1842 by Ernst August King of Hannover in memory of his deceased wife

Die historische Wandelhalle dient heute Konzertveranstaltungen und beherbergt zudem ein Café-Restaurant
Today, the historic pump room is used for concerts and also houses a coffee shop-restaurant

A completely different world presents itself at Bad Rehburg that, after the discovery of healing water in 1690, initially attracted members of the Hannoverian nobility searching for relief of their ailments. From the mid-18th century, it was expanded to the baths of the Hannoverian Court and flourished in particular in the Romantic period. Bathhouse, well house, pump room and other facilities were built, and the Hannoverian court gardeners landscaped the gardens and parks directing the views towards Lake Steinhude. In the spa facilities, nobility and wealthy bourgeoisie met so casually as nowhere else. As a young man, Johann Georg Kestner, who was to become archivist of Hannover (and is known as the husband of Lotte from Goethe's "Werther"), experienced "true fountain freedom" here. Following its restoration, Bad Rehburg, together with Hofgeismar, is considered the only remaining bathing facility from the Romanticist period in Germany. Spa life is realistically demonstrated at a small bath museum. The existence of the bath, the natural beauty in the form of the Rehburg Mountains, the near Lake Steinhude, Scharnhorst School in Wunstorf and, last but not least, business opportunities in potash mining probably motivated the pharmacist Ernst Georg Jünger to move to Rehburg-Stadt in 1907. His sons Ernst and Friedrich Georg were to become well-known writers, especially Ernst who achieved fame with his novel "Storm of Steel" about the First World War. However, those who are interested in life in the Lake Steinhude region during the Wilhelminian era, should read Friedrich Georg's childhood memories "Grüne Zweige" ("Green Twigs").

Winzlar/Rehburg-Loccum

Text: Klaus Fesche

Im Südosten des Landkreises Nienburg, einem Zipfel, der bis an das Steinhuder Meer reicht, befindet sich das Dorf Winzlar, das seit der Gebietsreform 1974 zur Stadt Rehburg-Loccum gehört. Bereits in der Bronzezeit lebten im Gebiet des heutigen Dorfes Menschen – so jedenfalls lässt es sich aus hiesigen Bodenfunden deuten. Die in einem Frauengrab gefundenen Gegenstände – Knochen, eine Nadel und ein Bronzebecken – sind heute im Heimatmuseum Rehburg ausgestellt.

Erstmals urkundlich erwähnt wurde Winzlar, in dem heute gut 1 000 Einwohner leben, im Jahre 1196. Ganz in der Nähe, auf dem Haarberg, lagen im Mittelalter das Dorf Münchhausen und die gleichnamige Burg – Stammsitz des Adelsgeschlechts derer von Münchhausen, aus dem im 18. Jahrhundert der in der Literatur berühmte „Lügenbaron" hervorgegangen ist. Bald nach 1335 sind Dorf und Burg wüst gefallen, wohl nach einem kriegerischen Konflikt. Angeblich unter Verwendung von Steinen dieser Burg ließen die von Münchhausen dann Mitte des 16. Jahrhunderts die Wasserburg Brokeloh (heute zu Landesbergen, ebenfalls im Landkreis Nienburg gelegen) errichten.

Die Lage Winzlars – halbkreisförmig vom Naturschutzgebiet Meerbruchwiesen umschlossen, nur etwa einen Kilometer vom Steinhuder Meer entfernt – ließ das Dorf auch bestens geeignet erscheinen, dort 1991 die „Ökologische Schutzstation Steinhuder Meer e.V." (ÖSSM) zu errichten, zumal dort ein altes Bauernhaus zur Verfügung stand. Hier wird seitdem von einem kompetenten Team, zu dem vier Wissenschaftler gehören, wichtige Naturschutz- und -bildungsarbeit geleistet. Im Gebäude der ÖSSM ist auch eine Ausstellung zur Entwicklung und Natur des Steinhuder Meeres zu besichtigen.

The village of Winzlar is situated to the southeast of the district of Nienburg, a strip of land that extends up to Lake Steinhude. Under the local government reform in 1974, it became part of the town of Rehburg-Loccum. Local archaeological finds indicate that people lived in the area of today's village already in the Bronze Age. Items found in a woman's grave – bones, a needle and a bronze basin – are on display at the Museum of Local History in Rehburg.

Winzlar, which today has a population of about 1,000, was first documented in 1196. On the nearby Haarberg Moutain, the village Münchhausen was situated in the Middle Ages, which included the castle of the same name. This used to be the residence of the aristocratic family of Münchhausen, and one of its members was the "Lying Baron", whose adventures are well known in literature. Soon after 1335, the village and the castle were destroyed, probably during an armed conflict. Legend has it that the Münchhausen family then used the stones of this castle to build the Brokeloh Water Castle in the mid-16th century (which today is Landesbergen, also situated in the district of Nienburg).

Winzlar's location – enclosed in a semicircle formed by the Meerbruch Meadows conservation area, only about one kilometre away from Lake Steinhude – made it the ideal place for the "Lake Steinhude Ecological Protection Station e.V."(ÖSSM), which moved into an old farmhouse there in 1991. Since then, a competent team that includes four scientists has been engaged in important conservation and education work. The building of the ÖSSM also houses an exhibition on the development and nature of Lake Steinhude.

Die Ökologische Schutzstation Steinhuder Meer (ÖSSM) in Winzlar und ihre Mitarbeiter von links nach rechts:
Oben: Daniel Towers (FÖJ), Alina Probst (FÖJ), Rebecca Rasche (BFD)
Unten: Thomas Brandt (wissenschaftlicher Leiter), Annika Ruprecht (wissenschaftliche Mitarbeiterin), Eva Lüers (wissenschaftliche Mitarbeiterin)
Nicht im Bild: Thomas Beuster (Geschäftsführer), Ann-Christin Röger (BFD)
Lake Steinhude Ecological Protection Station (ÖSSM) in Winzlar and its team, from left to right:
Top: Daniel Towers (FÖJ), Alina Probst (FÖJ), Rebecca Rasche (BFD)
Bottom: Thomas Brandt (scientific head), Annika Ruprecht (research assistant), Eva Lüers (research assistant)
Not pictured: Thomas Beuster (managing director), Ann-Christin Röger (BFD)

Ein für Winzlar typischer Bauernhof. Interessant ist das Schild „Milch-Bankenviertel", über das der Autor bei seinen Foto-Streifzügen stolperte. Dieses Schild weist auf früher dort stehende Bänke hin, die für den An- und Abtransport der Milchkannen genutzt wurden
A typical Winzlar farm. Note the interesting sign that translates "milk bank quarter", spotted by the author on his photo expeditions. This sign points to banks, which stood here in the past and which were used for delivering and collecting the milk churns

Münchehagen

Text: Klaus Fesche

Schon der Ortsname lässt Besuchern Assoziationen an längst vergangenen Zeiten hervorrufen, denn er weist auf die Loccumer Mönche hin, die hier eine eingehegte Siedlung anlegten. Und dass hier zu Zeiten des Dreißigjährigen Krieges grausame Hexenprozesse wüteten, im Zuge derer sieben Frauen verbrannt wurden, vervollständigt das Bild.
Doch das, wofür Münchehagen überregional bekannt ist, ist noch unendlich viel älter als Hexenwahn und marodierende Mönche: Es wurden die Fußspuren von Dinosauriern gefunden, die hier vor rund 140 Millionen Jahren in den Boden getreten worden sind und sich wundersamerweise bis heute erhalten haben.

Already the name of the town evokes associations in the visitors of a time long past, as it refers to the monks of Loccum, who founded an enclosed settlement here. And the fact that, in the days of the Thirty Years War, cruel witch trials were held here, during which seven women were burned, completes the picture. But what Münchehagen is well-known for beyond the borders of the region, is far older than witchcraft and marauding monks: Here, the footprints of dinosaurs were found. They were stamped into the soil about 140 million years ago and have miraculously been preserved.

Langhalsdinosaurier: Verursacher der Dinosaurierfährten von Münchehagen
Long-necked dinosaur: It left behind the dinosaur tracks of Münchehagen

Rechts: Über 200 versteinerte Dinosaurierspuren sind auf dem Naturdenkmal „Dinosaurierspuren von Münchehagen" zu bestaunen. Die Fährtenhalle schützt diese einmaligen Zeitzeugen vor der Zerstörung durch Witterungseinflüsse
Right: Over 200 fossilized dinosaur tracks are on display at the natural monument "Dinosaur Tracks of Münchehagen". In the track hall, these unique witnesses of ancient times are protected from weather

Diplodocus-Herde auf dem Naturdenkmal Dinosaurierfährten
A herd of Diplodocus at the natural monument of dinosaur tracks

Die Münchehagener evangelische Kirche wurde 1713 erbaut
The Protestant church of Münchehagen was built in 1713

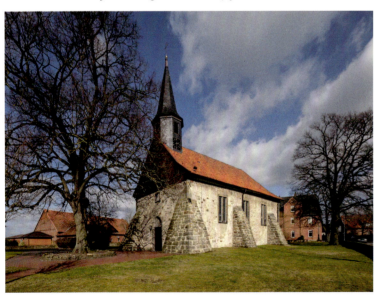

Diese 1980 gefundenen Saurierfährten waren Anlass, einen „Dinopark" zu errichten, der seither Hunderttausenden von Besuchern – Schulklassen, Familien und anderen Dinofans – einen eindrucksvollen Ausflug in die Erdgeschichte ermöglicht hat. Besonders anschaulich, vor allem für Kinder, ist das Freilichtmuseum wegen der mehr als 230 lebensgroßen Modelle von Tyrannosaurus rex, Archaeopteryx, Urzeitlibelle, Mammut und anderen längst ausgestorbenen Tierarten, die auf einem zweieinhalb Kilometer langen Rundweg bestaunt werden können. Das größte dieser Modelle, das eines Seismosaurus, ist nicht weniger als 45 Meter lang. Ergänzt wird der Park durch eine 3.500 Quadratmeter große Halle, in der die konservierten Spuren zu sehen sind. Aber auch als Forschungs- und Kompetenzzentrum für die Präparation von Fossilien ist die Einrichtung international anerkannt und wurde 2006 als „Nationaler Geotop" ausgezeichnet.

These dinosaur tracks, discovered in 1980, presented an opportunity for building a "Dinosaur Park". Since then, hundreds of thousands of visitors – school classes, families and other dino fans – have made the impressive trip into geological history. In particular children enjoy the open air museum, where more than 230 life-size models of Tyrannosaurus rex, Archaeopteryx, prehistoric dragonfly, mammoth and other extinct species are on display along a two and a half kilometre long trail. The largest of these models, showing a Seismosaurus, is no less than 45 metres long. The park also includes a 3,500 square metre hall in which the preserved footprints can be viewed. The establishment is internationally acclaimed as a research and competence centre for the preparation of fossils and received the "National Geotop" award in 2006.

Auch das Modell eines Mammuts ist im Dinopark zu bestaunen
A mammoth is one of the models displayed in the Dino Park

Mardorf

Text: Klaus Fesche

Der heutige Ortskern Mardorfs ist nicht der historische: Ursprünglich lag das 1173 erstmals erwähnte Dorf (wie der Ortsname auch nahelegt: "Mar-" ist mit "Meer-" zu übersetzen) direkt am Ufer des Steinhuder Meeres. Doch nach dem Dreißigjährigen Krieg war ein Großteil des alten Mardorfs, dessen Bewohner wohl noch vom Fischfang gelebt hatten, zerstört. Der Wiederaufbau geschah einige Hundert Meter weiter nördlich, abseits vom Ufer des Sees, dessen Wasserspiegel und Fischbesatz die Schaumburger bzw. Steinhuder erfolgreich für sich beanspruchten.

So mussten sich die Mardorfer jahrhundertelang mit der Landwirtschaft begnügen, und wegen der kargen, ertragsarmen Böden gelang das mehr schlecht als recht.

Eine Wende brachte erst die Zeit der Hochindustrialisierung im Kaiserreich, die auch den modernen Tourismus hervorbrachte. Am Nordufer des Steinhuder Meeres zeigte sich der Fremdenverkehr zunächst in Gestalt des „unberührte Natur"-suchenden Stadtflüchters. Vor dem Ersten Weltkrieg waren die Besucherzahlen des „Weißen Berges" (der großen Sanddüne im Nordwesten) oder der „Schwarzen Berge" (ältere, bewachsene Dünen) noch sehr überschaubar, doch bereits kurz danach fasste hier ein Massentourismus Fuß, der alles andere als naturnah war.

Today's town centre is not the historical centre of Mardorf: Originally, the village, which was first mentioned in 1173, was situated (as the town's name suggests: "Mar" is "Meer") directly on the shores of Lake Steinhude. However, after the Thirty Years' War, a major part of the old Mardorf, whose inhabitants had probably lived from fishing, was destroyed. The town was then reconstructed a few hundred metres further north, away from the shore of the lake. The population of Schaumburg and Steinhude was successful in securing the water and the fish in it for themselves.

As a result, the residents of Mardorf had to live of agriculture, which was very difficult in view of the poor quality of the soil.

The turning point came only in the period of high industrialisation during the German Empire, which also saw the beginnings of modern tourism. Initially, tourists visiting the northern shore of Lake Steinhude were mainly city dwellers searching for "pristine nature". While the number of visitors to the "White Mountain" (the large sand dune in the northwest) or the "Black Mountains" (older, overgrown dunes) was relatively manageable before the First World War, only shortly afterwards the area recorded a mass tourism that was anything but close-to-nature.

Am schönsten sind Spaziergänge am leeren Strand außerhalb der Saison – auch wenn es nur der kurze Weg ins Wasser ist
Leisurely walks along the deserted beach are best enjoyed out of season – even if it is just a short way into the water

Wikipedia sagt: „Ein Pilzkiosk ist ein für die 1950er Jahre typisches Kioskgebäude in Form eines Fliegenpilzes, das ursprünglich für die Verkaufsförderung von Milch und Milchprodukten als „Milchpilz" entwickelt wurde." ... und steht in diesem Falle an der Promenade in Mardorf
We find the following explanation in the German Wikipedia article: "Mushroom kiosks in the shape of a fly agaric were quite common selling booths in the 1950s. They were originally designed as "milk mushrooms" for promoting the sale of milk and dairy products." ... This one can be found on the promenade in Mardorf

Erbaut wurde das Gebäude als Schule 1842. Nachdem 1959 eine neue Schule gebaut worden war, wurde es größtenteils als Wohngebäude genutzt. Im Jahre 2002 hatte die heutige Betreiberin des Restaurants die Idee, die „Alte Schule" zumindest teilweise wieder zu nutzen und eröffnete im darauffolgenden Jahr darin ein Hotel und Restaurant, das heute weit über die Grenzen Mardorfs bekannt ist
The house was built as a school in 1842. After a new school was built in 1959, it was mostly used as a dwelling. In 2002, the current manager of the restaurant had the idea to use parts of the "Old School" and opened a hotel and restaurant there in the following year, which is known far beyond the borders Mardorf

Tausende von Badegästen am „Wannsee von Hannover" hinterließen deutlich sichtbare Naturschäden, und als Reaktion darauf entwickelte sich eine erste Naturschutzbewegung am Steinhuder Meer. Es entstanden aber auch legendäre gastronomische Ziele wie die „Alte Moorhütte" und die „Blaue Grotte", wo Segler, Wanderer und Badetouristen einkehren konnten.
Nach dem Zweiten Weltkrieg entwickelte sich das Mardorfer Ufer gar zum „größten Campingplatz Norddeutschlands", ebenso schossen schnell wachsende Wochenendhaus-Siedlungen aus dem Boden. Parallel ließen sich hier zahlreiche Segelclubs nieder, sichtbar an vielen, lang ins Meer ausgreifenden Bootstegen.
Dem Verband Großraum Hannover gelang es seit den 1960er Jahren, Ordnung in den Wildwuchs zu bringen. Heute ist der Tourismus aus Mardorf nicht mehr wegzudenken, und eine breite Palette von Angeboten bietet sich den Erholung suchenden Menschen: Vom Golfplatz über den

langen Badestrand bis zum Revier für Kitesurfer fehlt fast nichts – außer Möglichkeiten zum Bergsteigen!

Thousands of bathers at the "Wannsee of Hannover" left clearly visible damage to nature. This prompted the establishment of the first conservation movement at Lake Steinhude. However, also legendary gastronomic destinations such as the "Alte Moorhütte" ("Old Moor Hut") and the "Blaue Grotte" ("Blue Grotto") were founded, which are frequented by sailors, hikers and beach tourists. After the Second World War, the shore in Mardorf developed into the "biggest camping site in Northern Germany", while the number of weekend home settlements also grew rapidly. At the same time, numerous sailing clubs were established, obvious from the many landing stages that reach far into the lake.

In the 1960s, the Association of Greater Hannover succeeded in putting an end to uncontrolled growth. Today, Mardorf would be unimaginable without tourism; recreation seekers can choose from a wide offer and will find almost anything here, from the golf course

and the long beach through to a kite surfing area – except for mountain climbing!

Der Golfpark Steinhuder Meer. Der Blick vom 13. Grün auf die Wastearea von Bahn 15
Lake Steinhude golf course. The view from the 13th green onto the waste area of fairway 15

So ähnlich sieht es ein Seeadler oder anderer Vogel, wenn er die Bahn 14 vom Golfpark Steinhuder Meer überfliegt
This is more or less the view a sea eagle or any other bird has, when flying over the fairway 14 of Lake Steinhude golf course

Neustadt am Rübenberge

Text: Klaus Fesche

Stolze 800 Jahre zählt Neustadt a.Rbge, legt man die es zuerst erwähnende Urkunde zugrunde. Jedenfalls wurde die „nova civitas" von den Grafen von Wölpe an einem Leineübergang angelegt, eine Lage, die den Stadtherren gute Einnahmen verschaffte, denn die Leine war im Mittelalter noch schiffbar.
1302 verkauften die Grafen dann die Stadt an die Herzöge von Braunschweig-Lüneburg, also ans Welfenhaus, und ein Zweig dieser Dynastie machte Neustadt zeitweise gar zur Residenzstadt – die Fürsten von Calenberg, Erich der I. und dessen Sohn Erich II. Dieser ließ ab 1573 das Schloss Landestrost im Renaissancestil errichten und zudem Schloss und Stadt von einer großen Festungsanlage umgeben, deren Bastionen teilweise noch heute zu besichtigen sind. Erich II. ist aber auch für eine Reihe von Hexenprozessen berüchtigt, die er während der langjährigen Streitigkeiten mit seiner Frau Sidonie anstrengte und im Zuge derer mehrere Frauen Folter und Feuertod erleiden mussten.
Als werde die Stadt dafür gestraft, begann bald darauf für Neustadt – ähnlich wie für Wunstorf – eine Zeit der Krisen und Katastrophen, deren Höhepunkt der verheerende Stadtbrand von 1727 war. Noch im selben Jahr begann der planmäßige Wiederaufbau, finanziell unterstützt vom hannoverschen Kurfürsten und König von Großbritannien, Georg I.
Der Eisenbahnanschluss 1847 brachte einige Industrie in die Stadt, insbesondere die allerdings kurzlebige Neustädter Hütte oder die erfolgreichere Maschinenfabrik

According to the deed that first mentioned Neustadt a.Rbge, the town is respectable 800 years old. The "nova civitas" was founded by the Counts of Wölpe near a crossing over the Leine River, and as ships could still navigate on the river in the Middle Ages this location generated a good income for the sovereigns.
In 1302, the counts sold the town to the Dukes of Brunswick-Lüneburg, i. e. to the House of Guelph. One branch of this dynasty, namely the Princes of Calenberg, Erich I. and his son Erich II, had their residence in Neustadt for a while. From 1573, however, the latter built Landestrost Castle in the Renaissance style and also erected a large fortress that surrounded the castle and the town. Parts of the bastions of the fortress are still visible today. Erich II. is notorious for a series of witch trials, which he instigated in many years of arguments with his wife Sidonie.
During these, several women were tortured and burnt at the stake. As if the town was punished for it, Neustadt – similar to Wunstorf – saw a period of crises and disasters that culminated in the devastating fire of 1727. Reconstruction began in the same year, funded by the Prince-Elector of Hannover and King of Great Britain, George I. The railway connection in 1847 brought some industries to the town, in particular the Neustadt iron works, which were, however, short-lived, or the successful machine factory Schlüter.

Das illuminierte Amtsgerichtsgebäude in Neustadt a.Rbge. zwischen Schloss Landestrost und dem Stadtzentrum mit der Liebfrauenkirche
The illuminated district court building in Neustadt a.Rbge., situated between Landestrost Castle and the town centre with the Church of Our Lady

Schlüter. Dennoch blieb Neustadt, seit Jahrhunderten auch braunschweig-lüneburgischer Amtssitz, ab 1885 Kreisstadt mit Amtsgericht eher Verwaltungstadt als Wunstorf mit seinem günstigeren Bahnanschluss. Das Amtsgericht liegt passenderweise an der Ludwig-Ennecerus-Straße, benannt nach einem aus Neustadt stammenden Mitautoren des Bürgerlichen Gesetzbuches. Durch die Gebietsreform 1974 wuchs Neustadt auf eine Fläche von 357 Quadratkilometern an und wurde damit eine der größten Städte Deutschlands, allerdings bei heute mit 45 000 Einwohnern sehr dünn besiedelt. Das Stadtgebiet erstreckt sich vom kleinen Stöckendrebber im Norden bis zum 25 Kilometer südlicher reizvoll an einer Leineschleife gelegenen Bordenau, dem Geburtsort Scharnhorsts.

Insgesamt hat Neustadt einen sehr ländlichen Charakter, viele der eingemeindeten Dörfer haben weniger als 1 000 Einwohner, Averhoy gar weniger als 100.

Nevertheless, Neustadt, which for centuries had been used as headquarters of the administration of Braunschweig-Lüneburg, from 1885 district town with district court, remained an administrative town, unlike Wunstorf with its more favourable railway connection. Fittingly, the district court is based in Ludwig Ennecerus Street, named after one of the co-authors of the German Civil Code, who came from Neustadt. Following the local government reform in 1974, Neustadt expanded to an area of 357 square kilometres and thus became one of the largest towns in Germany, sparsely populated though, with just 45,000 inhabitants. The town area extends from the little Stöckendrebber in the north to Bordenau, which is attractively situated at a sinuosity of the Leine River 25 km to the south. It is the birthplace of General Scharnhorst.

Neustadt exudes a very rural atmosphere, many of the incorporated villages have less than 1,000 inhabitants, Averhoy even less than 100.

Links: Die Liebfrauenkirche. Weißstörche haben sich als Kulturfolger dem Menschen eng angeschlossen und brüten wie das Storchenpaar in Neustadt oft in dessen Nähe

Left: The Church of Our Lady. Being synanthropes, white storks have developed a close association with people and often breed near them, like this pair in Neustadt

Oben: Ein prächtiger Bronzelöwe ziert die Neustädter Löwenbrücke über die Leine. Früher galt der Löwe – der auch im Stadtwappen zu finden ist – den Landesherren als Zeichen der Macht

Top: A magnificent bronze lion adorns the Neustadt Lion Bridge that crosses the Leine River. In the old days, rulers regarded the lion – which can also be found in the coat of arms – as a symbol of power

Das Schloss Landestrost ist kultureller Mittelpunkt der Stadt und beherbergt neben Stadtbibliothek und Torfmuseum auch das Archiv der Region Hannover. Seine Räumlichkeiten ermöglichen daneben auch attraktive Ausstellungen und Kulturveranstaltungen. Eine Besonderheit findet sich noch in den Kellergewölben des Schlosses – die nördlichste Sektkellerei Deutschlands. Von dem Schloss umgebenden Amtsgarten aus, den ein bemerkenswerter Hainbuchen-Laubengang ziert, hat man einen schönen Blick auf die Windungen der Leine. Gegenüber der wuchtigen Liebfrauenkirche im nahen Stadtzentrum befindet sich zudem das Neustädter Museum, in dem regelmäßig Sonderausstellungen zu lokalhistorischen oder kulturgeschichtlichen Themen gezeigt werden. Vor allem durch die Moorstraße nach Mardorf ist Neustadt gut ans Steinhuder Meer angebunden.

The Landestrost Castle is the cultural centre of the town. Apart from the town library and the peat museum, it also houses the archive of the Hannover Region. Furthermore, attractive exhibitions and cultural events are organized on the premises. The vaults of the castle house another attraction – the most northerly sparkling wine production in Germany. From the administrative gardens that surround the castle and that include a remarkable hornbeam-lined pergola, visitors have a beautiful view of the bends of the Leine River. Opposite the massive Church of Our Lady in the nearby town centre, the Neustadt Museum is located where special exhibitions on local-historic or cultural-historical topics are organized on a regular basis. The Moorstraße towards Mardorf provides a good connection for Neustadt with Lake Steinhude.

Oben und rechts: Schloss Landestrost ist heute ein Kulturzentrum und beherbergt das Archiv der Region Hannover, ein Torfmuseum und einen schönen Rittersaal für kulturelle Veranstaltungen. Auch Volkshochschule und Stadtbibliothek sind hier zu finden
Above and right: Landestrost Castle is now a cultural centre and houses the archives of the Hannover Region, a peat museum and a beautiful knight's hall that is used for cultural events. An adult education centre and the town's library can also be found here

Zu Füßen von Schloss Landestrost windet sich die Leine durch Neustadt
At the foot of Landestrost Castle, the Leine River meanders through Neustadt